Leader's Guide

HALF

Changing Your Life Plan
from Success to Significance

TIME

Leader's Guide

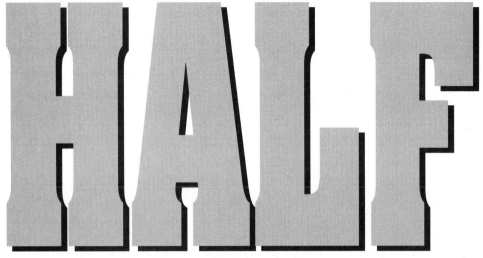

HALF

*Changing Your Life Plan
from Success to Significance*

TIME

Five Sessions Based on the Best-Selling Book by

BOB BUFORD

Leader's Guide written with Stephen and
Amanda Sorenson

ZondervanPublishingHouse
Grand Rapids, Michigan

Contents

Introduction

Something different begins to happen in our lives as we approach the special time that Bob Buford calls *halftime*. It's as if we've come to the end of a row and can't plow any further. It's time for something new. And it can be unsettling. That's why Buford's first book, *Halftime*, and his later book, *Game Plan*, have struck a chord with people from many walks of life and socioeconomic backgrounds who find themselves asking questions about the meaning and significance of their lives.

This study series is based on Buford's metaphor of a football game or any sport that divides its play into two halves. The playing field is the world in which we live. Halftime is the opportunity, after some of our life has passed, to evaluate what has taken place during the first half and to choose which new goals and dreams we may want to pursue during the second half of our lives.

The reality of the game of life, whether we like to admit it or not, is that the clock is running. What once looked like an eternity ahead of us is now within reach. Although we don't fear the end of the game, we do want to make sure that we finish well, that we leave something behind that no one can take away from us. This video and discussion series will help us discover significance and chart a course that will make the second half of our lives the best half.

How to Use This Guide

This Leader's Guide is divided into five sessions of approximately fifty-five minutes in length. Session 2 has two video presentations; the other sessions each have one video presentation.

Although this guide can be used for individual study, it is designed for groups. It can be used for retreats, in small group studies, and as a Sunday school elective. Growing into the second half of life takes more than a desire. A small group provides the essential elements of accountability, discipline, and authenticity.

BEFORE THE FIRST SESSION

- Watch the videotaped presentation.
- Obtain the necessary Participant's Guides for all participants.
- Make sure you have the items mentioned below.

Leader's Necessities

For each session, you will need:

- Leader's Guide
- Bible (Old and New Testaments)
- Video player, monitor, stand, extension cord, etc.
- Videotape(s)
- Watch or clock with which to monitor time
- Extra pens or pencils if needed by participants

Note: For some sessions, you may also want to use an overhead projector, chalkboard, or markerboard.

Participant's Necessities

For each session, each participant will need:

- Participant's Guide
- Bible (Old and New Testaments)
- Pen or pencil

DIRECTIONS FOR THE LEADER

These directions are enclosed in shaded boxes and are not meant to be read to the group.

SUPPLEMENTARY MATERIALS

The *Halftime Drills,* which supplement the sessions, are exercises that individuals can complete on their own. *Halftime Perspectives* are supplementary information that will enhance and deepen participants' understanding of the halftime process.

If your group has more time available than the typical one-hour time slot, you may include the Halftime Drills and the Halftime Perspectives as part of your sessions. Otherwise, these are available as additional resources for participants who want to deepen their study on their own.

The *Halftime Clips* and *Halftime Tips* are significant quotations that explain, supplement, and enhance the halftime process. Many of these quotations would also be excellent discussion starters.

Throughout the sessions, *Possible Answers* follow key, group-related questions for participants. The Possible Answers will provide you with an inkling of the responses participants may give and also guide you in emphasizing key points.

HOW EACH SESSION IS DIVIDED

Each session is divided into six main parts: *Before You Lead, Introduction, Video Presentation, Group Discovery, Action Points,* and *Closing Meditation.* (Session 2, the only session to have two video presentations, contains the same parts but is organized a little differently.)

A brief explanation of each part follows.

1. Before You Lead

Synopsis

Summarizes, for the leader, the material presented in each session.

Key Points of This Session

Highlights the key points the leader will want to emphasize.

Session Outline

Provides an overview of the session's content and activities.

Materials

Summarizes the essential materials the leader will need.

2. Introduction

Welcome

Welcomes participants to the session.

What's to Come

A brief, introductory summary you may choose to use.

Questions to Think About

Designed to help everyone begin thinking about the themes that will be covered in the session. A corresponding page is included in the Participant's Guide.

3. Video Presentation

During this time, the leader and participants will watch the video segment and write down appropriate notes. (The video presentation for session 2 is in two parts.) Key themes are highlighted in the guide books.

4. Group Discovery

In this longer section, the leader will guide participants in thinking through themes and issues related to halftime, including what is presented in each video segment. You may want to use the material in the order in which it is presented. Feel free to amplify various points with your own material or illustrations.

The Leader's Guide includes copies of the corresponding *Group Discovery* pages found in the Participant's Guide. Space is also provided in which to write additional planning notes. Having the Participant's Guide pages in front of you allows you to view the pages the participants are seeing as you talk without having to hold two books at the same time. It also lets you know where the participants are in their book when someone asks you a question.

Some groups will discuss questions more freely and extensively than others. Questions are provided to keep discussion moving with less expressive groups. If you are leading an expressive group and find that you cannot complete as many questions as are provided, select the key questions you would like your group to explore.

Video Highlights

As time permits, use these questions with the entire group. They will guide participants in verbally responding to the key points and themes covered in each video segment.

Large Group Exploration

During this time, you will guide the group in exploring a key theme or topic of the session. Often a few introductory sentences are provided that set the stage for discussion. Various approaches are used to stimulate learning and discussion. Sometimes questions are offered. Other times, participants will work together to complete charts or discuss Bible passages.

Pause for Personal Reflection, which comes at the end of Large Group Exploration, gives participants the opportunity to apply what they've just discovered to their lives. During this time, participants should not talk among themselves.

Small Group Exploration

For this exercise, if your group has more than seven participants you will break the group into small groups (three to five people), each of which will explore the topic or theme provided. If your group has seven participants or fewer, keep your group together.

If you wish, you can use the brief, introductory material that precedes the featured Small Group Exploration topic. If time allows, explore each question as a group. Or, to cover more ground, ask one person in each group to distribute questions or verses among participants. In either case, participants will write down answers to the questions.

At the close of Small Group Exploration, the Pause for Personal Reflection section gives participants a few moments to think through questions that encourage them to apply what they've just discovered to their lives. This is to be a quiet time, not a sharing time.

Group Discussion

During this time, the entire group will come together to explore additional halftime questions that wrap up the session. As time allows, feel free to use the material as is—or adapt it even more closely to the needs of your group.

5. Action Points

At this time, you'll summarize key points (provided for you) with the entire group. The application-oriented questions will encourage participants to act on what they have learned.

6. Closing Meditation

Close the session using the prayer provided. Or adapt the prayer to fit the particular needs of your group.

TIPS FOR LEADING AND PROMOTING GROUP DISCUSSION

1. Allow group members to participate at their comfort level. Not everyone needs to answer every question.

2. Ask questions with interest and warmth, then listen carefully to individual responses. Remember: it is important for participants to think through the questions and ideas presented as part of their halftime process. The *process* is more important than specific answers, which is why *possible* answers are provided.

3. Be flexible. Reword questions if you wish. Choose to spend more time on a topic. Add or delete questions to accommodate the needs of your group members—and your time frame.

4. Suggest that participants take time to explore any supplementary material that time did not permit them to explore within a session and to review previous sessions. This review will be particularly helpful if each session is being done weekly, for example, rather than all five sessions being done in a retreat setting.

5. Allow for (and expect) differences of opinion and experience. The halftime process is different for everyone.

6. Gently guide each participant into discussion. It may take some participants a while to feel comfortable enough to share.

7. Do not allow anyone to monopolize discussion. If such a situation arises, guide the discussion toward other people and perhaps speak to the person afterward about the importance of allowing everyone to share.

8. If a heated discussion begins on a theological topic, suggest that participants involved continue their discussion after the session is over.

9. Do not be afraid of silence. In fact, the Pause for Personal Reflection times are designed to encourage quiet, solitary reflection.

10. If you have time, read Bob Buford's books, *Halftime* and *Game Plan*, before or during these sessions. Obviously not everything in his books could be included in these sessions.

11. Monitor the time frames without being heavy-handed. Although it's important to keep each session moving, remember that the needs of your group may cause you to spend more or less time on a particular part of a session. Also, keep in mind that the content of each session has been carefully crafted, so try to keep to the allotted time

frames whenever possible. This will enable participants to cover all of the intended material.

12. If time allows, invite participants to talk with you before or after the sessions concerning their halftime process. What an encouragement you can be to them—by listening, sharing ideas, and sharing your experiences.

13. Approach these sessions with a joyful heart. Halftime is a wonderful opportunity—one that has guided a number of people toward their God-given callings.

14. As you work through this discussion guide and the sessions, be sure that you have found a person who will be your accountability partner. He or she will help hold your feet to the fire. This person should allow you to be honest, yet not judge you. Encourage participants to also select accountability partners—such as spouses or friends.

15. Last, but certainly not least, ask people to pray for you and your group as you go through these sessions. God wants to do great things in your lives!

1

Welcome to Halftime

BEFORE YOU LEAD

Synopsis

As recently as 1929, the average person in the United States had a life expectancy of fewer than fifty years. But today, most Americans and many people in other developed countries can expect to live twice as long as their great-grandparents. People today also have a greater number of options—financially, socially, vocationally, educationally.

Equally important, many of us are becoming what society calls successful. This does not necessarily mean we have accumulated a fortune or gained world renown. Success can also be defined in terms of achievement, such as attaining a degree of work-related status—something few people in previous generations had the opportunity to do. Successful people do not work merely to live, to pay the bills and survive long enough to retire. Those of us who are successful consider our jobs to be more than a way to buy our next meal. We expect to enjoy at least some aspects of our work, to become more proficient in our careers, and we often want to keep doing the work we enjoy even when we no longer have to do so for financial reasons.

At the same time we are attaining success, it's no secret that a growing number of us yearn for significance. Many of us between the ages of forty and seventy are discovering that our work isn't as fulfilling or challenging as it used to be. We realize it's time for a change, time to start a new season in life. In fact, we often find ourselves asking such new questions as:

- What do I want to do when I grow up?
- Have I really used my strengths, knowledge, and experience to the greatest advantage?
- I'm not ready to retire. Is it time for me to take on new challenges, maybe in a second career that allows me to express my values?
- Why am I so restless and dissatisfied with what I've accomplished so far? After all, I've met virtually all the goals I've wanted to achieve. Isn't there something more to life?

- Is what I'm doing meaningful to anybody?
- Could I start part of my life over and pursue things I have always dreamed of doing?

Bob Buford believes that God has placed each of us here on earth with a unique set of gifts and abilities, opportunities and relationships, inner desires and dreams, and a personal, God-given calling. So he considers these questions a wake-up call. And he has named the process by which we entertain these questions and seek to pursue our personal calling *halftime*.

Halftime occurs when the inner part of us questions the way things are—and wonders about the way things could be. When we look at where we've been and think about where we can go even though there's no clear road map. When we examine the question, "Why am I here?"

Halftime is the opportunity, after some of our life has passed, to evaluate what has taken place during the first half and to choose which new goals and dreams we may want to pursue during the second half of our lives.

In this first video segment, you'll be introduced to the halftime process and gain insights into the experiences of men and women who are undertaking exciting journeys from success to significance. There's no formula that leads people into halftime. As you'll see in the video, it is sometimes a yearning for significance, not just success, that comes only by finding one's specific calling. Terry Warren, by age forty-six, had accomplished virtually every goal he had set for himself, yet none of that seemed to matter anymore. Sometimes it's external circumstances. Chris Buehler, a church secretary, was thrown a curveball she couldn't hit when she was diagnosed with cancer. Sometimes it's an inner sense that things are out of balance. Lloyd Reeb realized that he could continue to pursue the same things he had pursued his entire life but that it was time to stop driving his agenda and join in God's agenda. And sometimes, as Bob Buford found, you just know that something different is happening in your life.

Regardless of what prompts us to begin the halftime process, the consequences of what we choose to do during halftime are great. The game is won or lost during the second half of our lives, not the first. The halftime experience makes the difference between whether we coast until the end of the game or live a vibrant second half.

Key Points of This Session

1. Today a growing number of men and women in midlife are asking themselves, "What do I want to do now that I've grown up? Is this all there is?" Bob Buford identifies this stage of life as halftime. It is the opportunity, after some of our life has passed, to evaluate what has taken place during the first half and to choose which goals and dreams we may want to pursue during the second half of our lives. Halftime is the start of an exciting journey that can take us past success and lead us toward significance.

2. Bob Buford believes that God has prepared each of us "to do a good work" and that when we reach the midpoint in life many of us can choose how we will spend the second part of our lives. Will we keep doing the same things in the same ways? Will we continue to pursue success and strive for more material possessions? Or will we courageously step out of the comfort zone and discover our God-given calling? Will we allow God to guide us toward something more? Will we use halftime to consciously evaluate where we have been and perhaps set our course in a new direction?

Session Outline (55 minutes)

   I. **Introduction** (5 minutes)
   Welcome
   What's to Come
   Questions to Think About

   II. **Video Presentation: "Welcome to Halftime"** (16 minutes)

   III. **Group Discovery** (28 minutes)
   Video Highlights (5 minutes)
   Large Group Exploration (9 minutes)
   Pause for Personal Reflection
   Small Group Exploration (9 minutes)
   Pause for Personal Reflection
   Group Discussion (5 minutes)

   IV. **Action Points** (5 minutes)

   V. **Closing Meditation** (1 minute)

Materials

You'll need a VCR, television set, and Bible, but no additional materials. Simply view the video segment prior to leading the session so you are familiar with its main points.

Session

1

Welcome to Halftime

The real test of a man [or woman] is not when he plays the role that he wants for himself, but when he plays the role destiny has for him.

Vaclav Havel

INTRODUCTION

minutes

Welcome

> Call the participants together. Welcome them to *Halftime* session 1, "Welcome to Halftime."

What's to Come

In this session, we'll be introduced to halftime, the process Bob Buford explores in his book of the same title. Many people, a few of whom we'll meet in this video, for one reason or another have been challenged or forced to seriously evaluate their life pursuits. As they have considered their accomplishments and looked toward the future, these people have found themselves asking such questions as, "What am I going to do when I grow up? Is this all there is? What's next?" As a result of facing these questions, rediscovering their deepest passions and how they are wired, and charting a new course for the second half of life, these men and women are experiencing a significance they never knew before.

Bob Buford believes that this journey toward significance is no accident. It is vitally important that people at the midpoint of their lives ask whether they are truly using their unique gifts, financial resources, abilities, time, knowledge, and opportunities in ways that will not only bring success to themselves but also make a significant impact in the lives of other people.

Session

1

Welcome to Halftime

The real test of a man [or woman] is not when he plays the role that he wants for himself, but when he plays the role destiny has for him.

Vaclav Havel

9

PLANNING NOTES

Questions to Think About

> **Have participants open their Participant's Guide to page 10.**
>
> **As time permits, ask two or more of the following questions and solicit responses from the participants.**

Let's begin this session by considering a few questions.

 1. How would you define *success?*

Possible Answers: Encourage participants to share honestly about what success looks like to them. Help them to consider a broad definition of success that includes financial security, personal accomplishment, peer recognition, meaningful family life, and breaking new ground professionally, etc.

 2. How would you describe the relationship between successfully earning a living and successfully using one's gifts, strengths, and abilities to create a significant life?

Possible Answers: Expect some diversity here. Some individuals may believe that success and significance are the same; others may believe that someone can earn a fine living but not have a significant life; and others may believe that earning a good living doesn't (or does) lead to much significance. Be prepared to point out that someone can be financially successful without necessarily investing his or her gifts, strengths, and abilities in a life of significance. Point out also that someone who doesn't earn much money may live a life of significance. Halftime is not just for influential, rich people; it's for everyone who desires to evaluate where he or she has been and to set a course toward significance.

 3. Which things do you consider to be truly significant—worth living or dying for?

Possible Answers: These may include making my family strong, accomplishing my goals, remaining committed to my spiritual beliefs, passing along values to my children, taking up a significant cause, better understanding God, winning in my career, helping less-fortunate people, etc.

Let's keep these ideas in mind as we view the video segment. There is space in your Participant's Guide for taking notes.

QUESTIONS TO THINK ABOUT

1. How would you define *success?*

2. How would you describe the relationship between success-fully earning a living and successfully using one's gifts, strengths, and abilities to create a significant life?

3. Which things do you consider to be truly significant—worth living or dying for?

PLANNING NOTES

VIDEO PRESENTATION: "Welcome to Halftime"

28

minutes

Leader's Video Observations
Halftime: Is it time for something new?

Incidents that encourage reevaluation

Questions of significance

Sensing the start of a new season

The two final questions:

What did you do about Jesus?

What did you do with what Jesus gave you—your aptitudes, abilities, experiences, and resources?

VIDEO NOTES

Halftime: Is it time for something new?

Incidents that encourage reevaluation

Questions of significance

Sensing the start of a new season

The two final questions:

What did you do about Jesus?

What did you do with what Jesus gave you—your aptitudes, abilities, experiences, and resources?

PLANNING NOTES

GROUP DISCOVERY

minutes

> If your group has seven or more members, use the **Video Highlights** (5 minutes) with the entire group, then complete the **Large Group Exploration** (9 minutes), then break into small groups of three to five people for the **Small Group Exploration** (9 minutes). Finally, bring everyone together for the closing **Group Discussion** (5 minutes).
>
> If your group has fewer than seven members, begin with the **Video Highlights** (5 minutes), then complete both the **Large Group Exploration** (9 minutes) and the **Small Group Exploration** (9 minutes) as a group. Wrap up your discovery time with the **Group Discussion** (5 minutes).

Video Highlights (5 minutes)

> As time permits, ask one or more of the following questions that directly relate to the video segment the participants have just seen.

 1. Do you now have a better idea of what halftime is? Let's come up with a working definition.

Possible Answers: Aspects of halftime may include a time to reevaluate priorities, a time when the daily circumstances of life aren't as challenging or fulfilling as they used to be, a time to chart a new course in life toward significance, a time to start using the gifts and abilities and knowledge one has been given in different ways, a time to listen to God in order to discover his calling for me, etc.

 2. Which of the people interviewed in the video segment described some of what you have felt or experienced? In what ways are they similar to or different from you?

Possible Answers: These will vary. The most important thing is to encourage people to begin thinking about their own lives—to increase the volume of the halftime issues that perhaps have been whispering in the background but have not been heeded.

 3. Which thoughts and emotions surfaced as you watched this video segment? What surprised you or stood out above the rest? Be honest!

Possible Answers: These may include feeling challenged to start thinking about some of the issues mentioned, being a bit angry at not having become more successful by this point in life, being excited about a truly significant future, wishing to chart a new direction in life but feeling it would be impossible to do so, being encouraged that people in midlife are able to

VIDEO HIGHLIGHTS

1. Do you now have a better idea of what halftime is? Let's come up with a working definition.

2. Which of the people interviewed in the video segment described some of what you have felt or experienced? In what ways are they similar to or different from you?

3. Which thoughts and emotions surfaced as you watched this video segment? What surprised you or stood out above the rest? Be honest!

PLANNING NOTES

make the second half of life better. The key here is to encourage participants to share of themselves and start considering the journey toward significance.

 4. Do you believe that the second half of our lives should be the best half—that it can be, in fact, a personal renaissance? Why or why not?

Possible Answers: These will vary. Some participants may see little ahead but retirement while others may be encouraged by the potential to use what they've been given during their second half. Still others, who may not have much materially, may be sparked to recognize that they too can live a life of significance.

HALFTIME CLIP

Halftime is the opportunity, after some of our life has passed, to evaluate what has taken place during the first half and to choose which new goals and dreams we may want to pursue during the second half of our lives.
—BOB BUFORD

Large Group Exploration (9 minutes)

Signals That Call for Our Attention

As we've seen, men and women who are in or are approaching halftime ask questions relating to their goals and life pursuits. They question perspectives and attitudes they have held for years. Previous goals and ways of doing things are no longer working as well as they used to. Let's explore some of the signals that indicate someone is in, or is approaching, halftime.

 1. What external circumstances can arise that force us to reevaluate our priorities during midlife?

Possible Answers: These may include illness—our own or that of our loved ones—the death of a close family member or friend, being fired or laid off from a job, facing a divorce initiated by a spouse, becoming addicted to alcohol or other substances, etc.

 2. What symptoms of internal restlessness may prompt us to reevaluate our priorities?

Possible Answers: suddenly waking up and realizing that we haven't done much that has impacted the lives of other people, feeling let down if what we

4. Do you believe that the second half of our lives should be the best half—that it can be, in fact, a personal renaissance? Why or why not?

HALFTIME CLIP

Halftime is the opportunity, after some of our life has passed, to evaluate what has taken place during the first half and to choose which new goals and dreams we may want to pursue during the second half of our lives.
—BOB BUFORD

LARGE GROUP EXPLORATION

Signals That Call for Our Attention
As we've seen, men and women who are in or are approaching halftime ask questions relating to their goals and life pursuits. They question perspectives and attitudes they have held for years. Previous goals and ways of doing things are no longer working as well as they used to. Let's explore some of the signals that indicate someone is in, or is approaching, halftime.

1. What external circumstances can arise that force us to reevaluate our priorities during midlife?

2. What symptoms of internal restlessness may prompt us to reevaluate our priorities?

3. How does the way we view our jobs today differ from the perspective of previous generations, particularly those of our grandparents or great-grandparents?

PLANNING NOTES

have is truly all there is, discovering that our careers aren't as rewarding as they once were, realizing that we have missed key times in our children's lives, realizing that our marriages aren't as fulfilling as we had hoped, feeling bored by activities or accomplishments that once recharged us, realizing that doing more of the same or acquiring more possessions will not satisfy us, etc.

 3. How does the way we view our jobs today differ from the perspective of previous generations, particularly those of our grandparents or great-grandparents?

Possible Answers: Today, many people build their lives around their careers. Our jobs have become a means of establishing our identity, giving us a place to belong, and affirming our significance. Years ago, most people viewed their jobs simply as a way to pay the bills. They received a sense of identity and belonging from their families, and their significance came from involvement in their respective communities.

 4. Describe, using your life or the life of someone you know, the visible signs that a person is not pleased with the way his or her life is going.

Possible Answers: These may include being dissatisfied with one's job, drinking too much (or other substance abuse), making a point of overdoing recreation, not being willing to push as hard to get ahead, checking want ads regularly, blaming other people because life isn't going as well as it should, being jealous of those who seem to have been able to get out of a rut and find new purpose in life, feeling trapped by circumstances, being viewed as successful but feeling unfulfilled, thinking that the best part of life is already over, wanting to spend more time being rather than doing, feeling that life is out of control, etc.

 5. Sometimes, when people feel bored or ineffective and wonder if this is all there is, they ignore the inner voice that urges them to stop and explore their unfulfilled dreams and deepest hopes. Why do people ignore the halftime issues, and what happens when they do?

Possible Answers: Some people are afraid of change or are pressured by peers or family members to maintain the status quo. Others choose to coast through the second half of life and lose their edge. Others may engage in a variety of diversions. For example, they may work even harder at their careers, divorce and remarry in order to regain a marital spark, buy even more toys, etc.

LARGE GROUP EXPLORATION

Signals That Call for Our Attention

As we've seen, men and women who are in or are approaching halftime ask questions relating to their goals and life pursuits. They question perspectives and attitudes they have held for years. Previous goals and ways of doing things are no longer working as well as they used to. Let's explore some of the signals that indicate someone is in, or is approaching, halftime.

1. What external circumstances can arise that force us to reevaluate our priorities during midlife?

2. What symptoms of internal restlessness may prompt us to reevaluate our priorities?

3. How does the way we view our jobs today differ from the perspective of previous generations, particularly those of our grandparents or great-grandparents?

4. Describe, using your life or the life of someone you know, the visible signs that a person is not pleased with the way his or her life is going.

5. Sometimes, when people feel bored or ineffective and wonder if this is all there is, they ignore the inner voice that urges them to stop and explore their unfulfilled dreams and deepest hopes. Why do people ignore the halftime issues, and what happens when they do?

Pause for Personal Reflection

Now it's time to pause to think quietly about the signals of coming change in our lives that demand our attention.

What signals in my life may be indicating that I am in, or am approaching, halftime? How might my spouse, a family member, or a close friend answer this question?

What gives my life meaning?

PLANNING NOTES

Pause for Personal Reflection

Now it's time to pause to think quietly about the signals of coming change in our lives that demand our attention.

- What signals in my life may be indicating that I am in, or am approaching, halftime? How might my spouse, a family member, or a close friend answer this question?
- What gives my life meaning?
- Which of my dreams and hopes haven't been fulfilled yet?
- What are the possible consequences if I were to reorder my life so that it would have greater significance?

Let participants know when there is one minute remaining.

HALFTIME CLIP

I knew what I believed, but I didn't really know what I planned to do about what I believed. I was gripped with an unformed but very compelling idea that I should make my life truly productive, not merely profitable.
—BOB BUFORD

Small Group Exploration (9 minutes)

What's Really Important?

Many years ago, the prophet Elijah powerfully brought God's judgment to bear on the false prophets of King Ahab of Israel. After God had demonstrated his power and the false prophets had been killed, King Ahab and his idolatrous wife, Jezebel, were angry. So Elijah fled for his life into the desert, where he evaluated his life and decided it was too tough to live. "I have had enough, Lord," he said. Then God spoke to him and asked him what he was doing in the desert. The prophet then spilled out his woes to God, and God responded.

 1. Read 1 Kings 19:11–16 and answer the following questions.

a. Often we pay attention to crises in our lives that force change, but we don't listen to the gentle whisper such as the one God provided Elijah. Why is it so hard for us to hear the whisper?

Possible Answers: We become too busy fending off crises; we are so used to doing everything at a frantic pace that we don't slow down to really evaluate things; we are so focused on being successful that we

4. Describe, using your life or the life of someone you know, the visible signs that a person is not pleased with the way his or her life is going.

5. Sometimes, when people feel bored or ineffective and wonder if this is all there is, they ignore the inner voice that urges them to stop and explore their unfulfilled dreams and deepest hopes. Why do people ignore the halftime issues, and what happens when they do?

Pause for Personal Reflection
Now it's time to pause to think quietly about the signals of coming change in our lives that demand our attention.

What signals in my life may be indicating that I am in, or am approaching, halftime? How might my spouse, a family member, or a close friend answer this question?

What gives my life meaning?

PLANNING NOTES

Which of my dreams and hopes haven't been fulfilled yet?

What are the possible consequences if I were to reorder my life so that it would have greater significance?

HALFTIME CLIP

I knew what I believed, but I didn't really know what I planned to do about what I believed. I was gripped with an unformed but very compelling idea that I should make my life truly productive, not merely profitable.
—BOB BUFORD

SMALL GROUP EXPLORATION

What's Really Important?
Many years ago, the prophet Elijah powerfully brought God's judgment to bear on the false prophets of King Ahab of Israel. After God had demonstrated his power and the false prophets had been killed, King Ahab and his idolatrous wife, Jezebel, were angry. So Elijah fled for his life into the desert, where he evaluated his life and decided it was too tough to live. "I have had enough, Lord," he said. Then God spoke to him and asked him what he was doing in the desert. The prophet then spilled out his woes to God, and God responded.

1. Read 1 Kings 19:11–16 and answer the following questions.

   a. Often we pay attention to crises in our lives that force change, but we don't listen to the gentle whisper such as the one God provided Elijah. Why is it so hard for us to hear the whisper?

   b. If we took more time to listen to our gentle whispers—the thoughts, feelings, inner promptings, words of God—that seem to come during times of reflection and reevaluation, what might the consequences be?

can't hear the whisper of significance; we often don't make time to listen to God, pray, and read the Bible; we may not believe that God will really reveal himself to us when we need help.

b. If we took more time to listen to our gentle whispers—the thoughts, feelings, inner promptings, words of God—that seem to come during times of reflection and reevaluation, what might the consequences be?

Possible Answers: We would be more in tune with God and what we are really thinking, the crises we experience wouldn't seem as overwhelming, we could better evaluate the direction of our lives, we would learn more about God and his love, etc.

 2. How important is it for us to have an eternal perspective through which to view the goals and activities—and even the crises—of our lives?

Possible Answers: It is very important. Without the perspective God alone can provide, we end up trying to determine truth on our own and establish our own standards. We end up being sucked into the vortex of the world's values rather than viewing what we do in light of God's purposes and destiny for our lives. We lose sight of the fact that God can turn what seem like bad things in our lives into positive things—in our lives, in the lives of other people around us.

 3. What does it really mean to "have it all," to be "successful" in this life?

Possible Answers: These will vary greatly. To some people, having it all means acquiring wealth, titles, possessions. To other people, it means developing deep relationships with family, friends, and God.

 4. Why do we tend to put off thinking about whether the way we are living life right now is the best way for us to live?

Possible Answers: We don't like to think that we may be missing out, that we may not be pursuing the best things. Also, many times there is no clear road map for the changes we may need to make in order to live life in ways that more closely fit our deepest desires and the knowledge, experience, and abilities we've been given by God.

 5. In John 10:10, Jesus preached that he, the Good Shepherd, had come to earth so that his followers, the sheep, might "have life, and have it to the full."

a. What do you think Jesus meant by having life "to the full"?

Possible Answers: These will vary but may include having everything one desires, having a full life, having a balanced life, having a significant inner life, being able to be joyful during both easy and difficult times, etc.

SMALL GROUP EXPLORATION

What's Really Important?

Many years ago, the prophet Elijah powerfully brought God's judgment to bear on the false prophets of King Ahab of Israel. After God had demonstrated his power and the false prophets had been killed, King Ahab and his idolatrous wife, Jezebel, were angry. So Elijah fled for his life into the desert, where he evaluated his life and decided it was too tough to live. "I have had enough, Lord," he said. Then God spoke to him and asked him what he was doing in the desert. The prophet then spilled out his woes to God, and God responded.

1. Read 1 Kings 19:11–16 and answer the following questions.

   a. Often we pay attention to crises in our lives that force change, but we don't listen to the gentle whisper such as the one God provided Elijah. Why is it so hard for us to hear the whisper?

   b. If we took more time to listen to our gentle whispers—the thoughts, feelings, inner promptings, words of God—that seem to come during times of reflection and reevaluation, what might the consequences be?

2. How important is it for us to have an eternal perspective through which to view the goals and activities—and even the crises—of our lives?

3. What does it really mean to "have it all," to be "successful" in this life?

4. Why do we tend to put off thinking about whether the way we are living life right now is the best way for us to live?

5. In John 10:10, Jesus preached that he, the Good Shepherd, had come to earth so that his followers, the sheep, might "have life, and have it to the full."

   a. What do you think Jesus meant by having life "to the full"?

PLANNING NOTES

b. Does this verse indicate that Jesus planned to lead his people to restrictive, unrewarding places, or to places of significance? Why?

Possible Answer: Jesus planned to lead his people to good places, to places where they would be nourished, etc.

Pause for Personal Reflection

Now it's time to pause to evaluate what's really important in our lives.

- What obstacles do I need to overcome in order to pay closer attention to my deepest longings? To the nudgings of God?
- In light of my definition of success, am I truly successful? Am I living life to the full? Why or why not?
- In what ways is my view of success changing? Is success as important to me as it once was?
- Am I living a balanced life? Which priorities deserve more time?

Let participants know when there is one minute remaining.

HALFTIME CLIP

When it comes to having a better second half than the first, it doesn't matter whether you're a millionaire CEO, a high-paid lawyer, or a teacher. What's important is that you start by discovering the way God built you so you can use your uniquely developed talents for him.

—BOB BUFORD

b. Does this verse indicate that Jesus planned to lead his people to restrictive, unrewarding places, or to places of significance? Why?

Pause for Personal Reflection

Now it's time to pause to evaluate what's really important in our lives.

What obstacles do I need to overcome in order to pay closer attention to my deepest longings? To the nudgings of God?

In light of my definition of success, am I truly successful? Am I living life to the full? Why or why not?

---

20   HALFTIME PARTICIPANT'S GUIDE

In what ways is my view of success changing? Is success as important to me as it once was?

Am I living a balanced life? Which priorities deserve more time?

HALFTIME CLIP

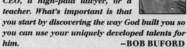

When it comes to having a better second half than the first, it doesn't matter whether you're a millionaire CEO, a high-paid lawyer, or a teacher. What's important is that you start by discovering the way God built you so you can use your uniquely developed talents for him.   **—BOB BUFORD**

PLANNING NOTES

Group Discussion (5 minutes)

Now it's time to wrap up our discovery time.

> **Give participants a moment to transition from their thoughtfulness and begin sharing their observations with the entire group. Use the following questions as discussion starters.**

 1. In what ways has what we have seen and discussed together today changed your definition of success?

 2. The Scripture passage about Elijah that we read in our small groups shows that just when Elijah thought he was spent, used up, and ready for permanent retirement, God spoke to him in a whisper and gave him something important to do! What does this story say to you as you approach halftime?

 3. So far, what are your thoughts about halftime? Are you encouraged? Apprehensive? Curious?

HALFTIME PERSPECTIVE

First-Half versus Halftime

The following chart, which is not pictured in the video, illustrates some of the differences that often exist between the first half of our lives and halftime.

Typical First-Half Pursuits and Challenges	Typical Halftime Questions and Issues
Obtaining an education.	What should I do with what I've learned? Have I done enough—in my family, my community, my church?
Getting married or building relationships with friends.	Am I able to devote time to the people who are most important to me? To help them become all they can be? To reach out to others?
Building a career and striving to move upward, trying to provide for the family. Having good intentions.	Are these long hours really worth the price? And now that I'm here, is this where I want to be? I want more than success; I want significance. I'm successful, fortunate, and yet frustratingly unfulfilled.
Acquiring material things to help make life's journey more comfortable.	May have lived more than half my life. What am I going to leave behind of lasting value? Do I really need more stuff?

continued on page 38...

GROUP DISCUSSION

1. In what ways has what we have seen and discussed together today changed your definition of success?

2. The Scripture passage about Elijah that we read in our small groups shows that just when Elijah thought he was spent, used up, and ready for permanent retirement, God spoke to him in a whisper and gave him something important to do! What does this story say to you as you approach halftime?

3. So far, what are your thoughts about halftime? Are you encouraged? Apprehensive? Curious?

HALFTIME PERSPECTIVE

First-Half versus Halftime

The following chart, which is not pictured in the video, illustrates some of the differences that often exist between the first half of our lives and halftime.

Typical First-Half Pursuits and Challenges	Typical Halftime Questions and Issues
Obtaining an education.	What should I do with what I've learned? Have I done enough—in my family, my community, my church?
Getting married or building relationships with friends.	Am I able to devote time to the people who are most important to me? To help them become all they can be? To reach out to others?
Building a career and striving to move upward, trying to provide for the family. Having good intentions.	Are these long hours really worth the price? And now that I'm here, is this where I want to be? I want more than success; I want significance. I'm successful, fortunate, and yet frustratingly unfulfilled.
Acquiring material things to help make life's journey more comfortable.	May have lived more than half my life. What am I going to leave behind of lasting value? Do I really need more stuff?
Juggling many priorities—how to be with friends and family yet expend oneself in the adventure of developing a career.	What's *really* important? Maybe it's time to take a breather and reevaluate things. How would I like my life to be different—if I'm really honest?

PLANNING NOTES

Juggling many priorities—how to be with friends and family yet expend oneself in the adventure of developing a career.	What's *really* important? Maybe it's time to take a breather and reevaluate things. How would I like my life to be different—if I'm really honest?
Experiencing pain: divorce, addiction, guilt, loneliness, wayward children, job loss, cancer, etc.	How can I use the great learning experiences I've had and wisdom I've gained to make a difference in this world—to draw me closer to people and to God?
Determining what I have to work with—my gifts, abilities, knowledge, experiences.	I know quite a bit about what I have to work with; now it's time to choose strategically how to use what I have.
Choosing challenges and new horizons that fit the game plan.	Now I can build on the past to create new challenges, new horizons that reflect my new goals and to discover what it means to be open to what God wants me to do.
Marching ahead, pursuing the goals, playing hard.	I just can't keep playing the game the way I've been playing. But I want the second half of my life to be even better than the first.
Trying to figure out what to believe spiritually. If this leads to becoming a Christian, then developing a belief system.	I want to figure out what to do with what I believe. I want my faith to be lived out through action that is built on my faith and beliefs.
Getting involved in activities and figuring out how life works.	I dare to believe that what I ultimately leave behind will be more important than anything I could have achieved during the first half of my life.

22   HALFTIME PARTICIPANT'S GUIDE

HALFTIME PERSPECTIVE

First-Half versus Halftime
The following chart, which is not pictured in the video, illustrates some of the differences that often exist between the first half of our lives and halftime.

Typical First-Half Pursuits and Challenges	Typical Halftime Questions and Issues
Obtaining an education.	What should I do with what I've learned? Have I done enough—in my family, my community, my church?
Getting married or building relationships with friends.	Am I able to devote time to the people who are most important to me? To help them become all they can be? To reach out to others?
Building a career and striving to move upward, trying to provide for the family. Having good intentions.	Are these long hours really worth the price? And now that I'm here, is this where I want to be? I want more than success; I want significance. I'm successful, fortunate, and yet frustratingly unfulfilled.
Acquiring material things to help make life's journey more comfortable.	May have lived more than half my life. What am I going to leave behind of lasting value? Do I really need more stuff?
Juggling many priorities—how to be with friends and family yet expend oneself in the adventure of developing a career.	What's *really* important? Maybe it's time to take a breather and reevaluate things. How would I like my life to be different—if I'm really honest?

SESSION ONE: Welcome to *Halftime*   25

Experiencing pain: divorce, addiction, guilt, loneliness, wayward children, job loss, cancer, etc.	How can I use the great learning experiences I've had and wisdom I've gained to make a difference in this world—to draw me closer to people and to God?
Determining what I have to work with—my gifts, abilities, knowledge, experiences.	I know quite a bit about what I have to work with; now it's time to choose strategically how to use what I have.
Choosing challenges and new horizons that fit the game plan.	Now I can build on the past to create new challenges, new horizons that reflect my new goals and to discover what it means to be open to what God wants me to do.
Marching ahead, pursuing the goals, playing hard.	I just can't keep playing the game the way I've been playing. But I want the second half of my life to be even better than the first.
Trying to figure out what to believe spiritually. If this leads to becoming a Christian, then developing a belief system.	I want to figure out what to *do* with what I believe. I want my faith to be lived out through action that is built on my faith and beliefs.
Getting involved in activities and figuring out how life works.	I dare to believe that what I ultimately leave behind will be more important than anything I could have achieved during the first half of my life.

PLANNING NOTES

ACTION POINTS

minutes

The following points are reproduced on page 24 of the Participant's Guide.

I'd like to take a moment to summarize the key points we explored today. After I have reviewed these points, I will give you a moment to consider what you will commit to do as a result of what you have discovered during this session.

Read the following points and pause afterward so participants can consider and write out their commitments.

 1. Today a growing number of men and women in midlife are asking themselves, "What do I want to do now that I've grown up? Is this all there is?" Bob Buford identifies this stage of life as *halftime*. It is the opportunity, after some of our life has passed, to evaluate what has taken place during the first half and to choose which goals and dreams we may want to pursue during the second half of our lives. Halftime is the start of an exciting journey that can take us past success and lead us toward significance.

   Most of us want not merely to be remembered but to be remembered for something significant. Here's one way to discover what is truly significant to you:

   Using just one phrase or sentence, write out what you would like written on your gravestone.

   Allow what you write to express the goals to which you will be committed until you rest beneath that gravestone, the purpose and passion that will characterize you from this day forward. (If you are not yet sure what to write, leave this question unanswered and come back to it later.)

 2. Bob Buford believes that God has prepared each of us "to do a good work" and that when we reach the midpoint of life many of us can choose how we will spend the second part of our lives. Will we keep doing the same things in the same ways? Will we continue to pursue success and strive for more material possessions? Or will we courageously step out of the comfort zone and discover our God-given calling? Will we allow God to guide us toward something more? Will we use halftime to consciously evaluate where we have been and perhaps set our course in a new direction?

ACTION POINTS

What will you commit to do as a result of what you have discovered during this session?

1. Today a growing number of men and women in midlife are asking themselves, "What do I want to do now that I've grown up? Is this all there is?" Bob Buford identifies this stage of life as *halftime*. It is the opportunity, after some of our life has passed, to evaluate what has taken place during the first half and to choose which goals and dreams we may want to pursue during the second half of our lives. Halftime is the start of an exciting journey that can take us past success and lead us toward significance.

   Most of us want not merely to be remembered but to be remembered for something significant. Here's one way to discover what is truly significant to you:

   Using just one phrase or sentence, write out what you would like written on your gravestone.

   Allow what you write to express the goals to which you will be committed until you rest beneath that gravestone, the purpose and passion that will characterize you from this day forward. (If you are not yet sure what to write, leave this question unanswered and come back to it later.)

2. Bob Buford believes that God has prepared each of us "to do a good work" and that when we reach the midpoint of life many of us can choose how we will spend the second part of our lives. Will we keep doing the same things in the same ways? Will we continue to pursue success and strive for more material possessions? Or will we courageously step out of the comfort zone and discover our God-given calling? Will we allow God to guide us toward something more? Will we use halftime to consciously evaluate where we have been and perhaps set our course in a new direction?

   Set aside at least one hour this week during which, away from most or all distractions, you can begin thinking about the following:

   1. Take an inventory of your unique gifts, resources, abilities, and experiences. (Examples might include the opportunity to influence people, time to pray, a strong character developed through suffering, a love for children, material resources, a level of expertise in a unique skill.)

PLANNING NOTES

Set aside at least one hour this week during which, away from most or all distractions, you can begin thinking about the following:

1. Take an inventory of your unique gifts, resources, abilities, and experiences. (Examples might include the opportunity to influence people, time to pray, a strong character developed through suffering, a love for children, material resources, a level of expertise in a unique skill.)

2. Now write down ways in which you might be able to use the above inventory during the second half of your life. Remember, no matter where you live, who you know, what you do, or how much money you make, God has a special calling for you to fulfill right where you are.

HALFTIME CLIP

I knew I was successful in my early thirties, and I was very troubled by it, of all things. I describe it in Halftime *as "success panic," where you actually get where you want to go! It's like a dog chasing a car and catching up with it and getting a bite of the tire—it's frightening in some ways. It caused me to sit down under a tree with my Daytimer and say, "What's really important? Is this it?"*
—BOB BUFORD

CLOSING MEDITATION

minute

Dear God, we thank you for the opportunity to begin thinking about the process of halftime and what it can mean for us and others we love. We've already made many life-related choices and accomplished various things. But now, we're exploring new territory. We're asking questions of ourselves that are not easy to answer, or even comfortable to ask. And we need your guidance and wisdom. Thank you for loving each of us, no matter who we are or where we've been. And please guide us as we seek to discover more about ourselves and the destinies you have for us that will bring significance. If we're feeling discouraged about where we are in life right now, remind us clearly that you are with us and can do way more than we would even ask for or anticipate. In your name we pray, amen.

2. Bob Buford believes that God has prepared each of us "to do a good work" and that when we reach the midpoint of life many of us can choose how we will spend the second part of our lives. Will we keep doing the same things in the same ways? Will we continue to pursue success and strive for more material possessions? Or will we courageously step out of the comfort zone and discover our God-given calling? Will we allow God to guide us toward something more? Will we use halftime to consciously evaluate where we have been and perhaps set our course in a new direction?

Set aside at least one hour this week during which, away from most or all distractions, you can begin thinking about the following:

1. Take an inventory of your unique gifts, resources, abilities, and experiences. (Examples might include the opportunity to influence people, time to pray, a strong character developed through suffering, a love for children, material resources, a level of expertise in a unique skill.)

2. Now write down ways in which you might be able to use the above inventory during the second half of your life. Remember, no matter where you live, who you know, what you do, or how much money you make, God has a special calling for you to fulfill right where you are.

HALFTIME CLIP

I knew I was successful in my early thirties, and I was very troubled by it, of all things. I describe it in Halftime as "success panic," where you actually get where you want to go! It's like a dog chasing a car and catching up with it and getting a bite of the tire—it's frightening in some ways. It caused me to sit down under a tree with my Daytimer and say, "What's really important? Is this it?"
—BOB BUFORD

PLANNING NOTES

Take Stock of Your First Half

The following questions may help you take stock of your first half as you prepare for a better second half.

1. For what do you want to be remembered? Describe how your life would look if it turned out just the way you wished.

2. How much money is enough? If you have more than enough, what purpose does the excess serve? If you have less than enough, what are you willing to do to correct that?

3. How do you feel about your career? Is this what you want to be doing with your life ten years from now?

4. Are you living a balanced life? Which important elements of your life deserve more time? Which elements would you like to eliminate?

5. Are you becoming the person you really want to be? If not, what are you willing to do about it?

6. What is the primary loyalty in your life?

7. Where do you seek inspiration and mentors for your life?

8. What kinds of relationships do you want with your family and friends?

9. What pursuits have dominated your life thus far? In what ways have you benefited from them? What have been the drawbacks?

10. If your life story to date indicates what lies ahead for you, what do you think your future holds?

HALFTIME DRILL

Take Stock of Your First Half

The following questions may help you take stock of your first half as you prepare for a better second half.

1. For what do you want to be remembered? Describe how your life would look if it turned out just the way you wished.

2. How much money is enough? If you have more than enough, what purpose does the excess serve? If you have less than enough, what are you willing to do to correct that?

3. How do you feel about your career? Is this what you want to be doing with your life ten years from now?

4. Are you living a balanced life? Which important elements of your life deserve more time? Which elements would you like to eliminate?

5. Are you becoming the person you really want to be? If not, what are you willing to do about it?

6. What is the primary loyalty in your life?

7. Where do you seek inspiration and mentors for your life?

8. What kinds of relationships do you want with your family and friends?

9. What pursuits have dominated your life thus far? In what ways have you benefited from them? What have been the drawbacks?

10. If your life story to date indicates what lies ahead for you, what do you think your future holds?

PLANNING NOTES

A Model for Our Spiritual Journey

In his first book, *Halftime*, Bob Buford uses the following baseball diagram to illustrate a person's spiritual journey. Perhaps it will help you clarify where you are—which base you are on or headed toward.

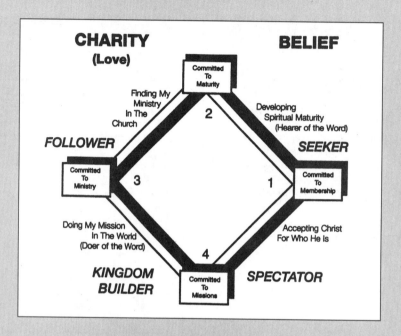

The First Half: Developing Faith and Belief

1. Getting to first base. Here, a spectator who has been on the sidelines accepts Jesus Christ for who he is through a simple act of faith. This act of faith changes the person from being a spectator to engaging his or her rational and emotional senses on the journey toward personal spiritual growth.

2. Moving to second base. The new Christian makes a commitment to developing spiritual maturity. This includes gaining an understanding of what faith in God really means. For many people, including Bob Buford, this part of the journey focuses on belief—the internally held belief system that grows the more they study the Bible and its unique truths concerning life and God.

Bob Buford, in *Halftime*, reported that George Gallup Jr. says 84 percent of Americans declare themselves to be Christians. Yet there doesn't seem to be corresponding evidence of Christlikeness in our society. Bob believes this is because many Christians are "stuck somewhere between first and second base."

The Second Half: Doing Good Works That Come from Faith and Belief

3. Reaching third base. Here, the person:

- Moves from spiritual maturity and developing a personal belief system to releasing seeds of creativity and energy that God has implanted in him or her.

HALFTIME PERSPECTIVE

A Model for Our Spiritual Journey

In his first book, *Halftime*, Bob Buford uses the following baseball diagram to illustrate a person's spiritual journey. Perhaps it may help you clarify where you are—which base you are on or headed toward.

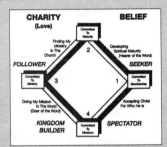

The First Half: Developing Faith and Belief

1. Getting to first base. Here, a spectator who has been on the sidelines accepts Jesus Christ for who he is through a simple act of faith. This act of faith changes the person from being a spectator to engaging his or her rational and emotional senses on the journey toward personal spiritual growth.

2. Moving to second base. The new Christian makes a commitment to developing spiritual maturity. This includes gaining an understanding of what faith in God really means. For many people, including Bob Buford, this part of the journey focuses on belief—the internally held belief system that grows the more they study the Bible and its unique truths concerning life and God.

Bob Buford, in *Halftime*, reported that George Gallup Jr. says 84 percent of Americans declare themselves to be Christians. Yet there doesn't seem to be corresponding evidence of Christlikeness in our society. Bob believes this is because many Christians are "stuck somewhere between first and second base."

The Second Half: Doing Good Works That Come from Faith and Belief

3. Reaching third base. Here, the person:

- Moves from spiritual maturity and developing a personal belief system to releasing seeds of creativity and energy that God has implanted in him or her.
- Waters and cultivates these seeds so they will become fruitful.
- Starts being committed to expressing love, to investing his or her gifts in service to other people. The resulting good works are an extension of the person's beliefs and give these beliefs integrity.
- Expresses his or her faith in Jesus by reaching out to other people, in the power of God, through a church or parachurch organization.
- Assumes individual responsibility, taking steps to be involved in people's lives.

4. Heading toward home plate. This person:

- Is discovering God's specific mission for him or her—what the Greeks called destiny.
- Is actively living out his or her faith in the everyday world.
- Is sharing the love and good news of Jesus with other people.
- Is committed to making a difference in the world through God's power.

PLANNING NOTES

- Waters and cultivates these seeds so they will become fruitful.
- Starts being committed to expressing love, to investing his or her gifts in service to other people. The resulting good works are an extension of the person's beliefs and give these beliefs integrity.
- Expresses his or her faith in Jesus by reaching out to other people, in the power of God, through a church or parachurch organization.
- Assumes individual responsibility, taking steps to be involved in people's lives.

4. Heading toward home plate. This person:

- Is discovering God's specific mission for him or her—what the Greeks called destiny.
- Is actively living out his or her faith in the everyday world.
- Is sharing the love and good news of Jesus with other people.
- Is committed to making a difference in the world through God's power.

Bob Buford, in *Halftime,* reported that George Gallup Jr. says 84 percent of Americans declare themselves to be Christians. Yet there doesn't seem to be corresponding evidence of Christ-likeness in our society. Bob believes this is because many Christians are "stuck somewhere between first and second base."

The Second Half: Doing Good Works That Come from Faith and Belief

3. Reaching third base. Here, the person:

- Moves from spiritual maturity and developing a personal belief system to releasing seeds of creativity and energy that God has implanted in him or her.
- Waters and cultivates these seeds so they will become fruitful.
- Starts being committed to expressing love, to investing his or her gifts in service to other people. The resulting good works are an extension of the person's beliefs and give these beliefs integrity.
- Expresses his or her faith in Jesus by reaching out to other people, in the power of God, through a church or parachurch organization.
- Assumes individual responsibility, taking steps to be involved in people's lives.

4. Heading toward home plate. This person:

- Is discovering God's specific mission for him or her—what the Greeks called destiny.
- Is actively living out his or her faith in the everyday world.
- Is sharing the love and good news of Jesus with other people.
- Is committed to making a difference in the world through God's power.

PLANNING NOTES

Session

2

Exploring Possibilities

BEFORE YOU LEAD

Synopsis

The video for this session is presented in two parts. A summary of each segment and the key points of this session follow.

Exploring Possibilities, Part 1 (12 minutes)

Bob Buford, the author of *Halftime,* introduces this video segment by saying that "a hero is someone who gives himself or herself over to something larger" than his or her personal concerns. What does being a hero have to do with our calling? Well, halftime is the time to begin making choices based on our calling and our commitment to a cause greater than ourselves.

The first video segment focuses on Bob and Tina Muzikowski, who as a result of their halftime evaluation, discovered their calling and put their faith into action. They became involved in a cause much larger than their personal concerns. With Tina's support, Bob Muzikowski started the Near West Little League, a baseball league that draws kids from Chicago's inner-city projects. It has become the biggest inner-city Little League in the United States.

Instead of throwing up their hands and thinking that inner-city problems were too large to tackle, Bob and Tina (and a few other people) choose to be personally involved. And that involvement has meant sacrifice. Bob and Tina moved their family from the suburbs into the inner city. Some of their friends pulled away. To give enough time to the youth involved in the Near West Little League, Bob scaled back his hours as a benefits planner and agent for Northwestern Mutual. He now makes half as much as he would ordinarily make, which he quickly adds "is still too much anyway."

Have Bob and Tina experienced setbacks in pursuing God's calling? You bet. Bob tells about a boy he coached for years who rode a bicycle that had no tires. He and another coach bought that young man new tires and fixed up the bicycle. It looked great! But soon afterward, the boy's grandmother asked Bob to identify the boy at the morgue. He had been shot and killed by kids who wanted his bicycle. Bob knows he's not going to win all the battles.

Despite the setbacks, Bob, Tina, and others like them are making a life-changing difference. They illustrate the change of heart essential to a successful second half. They are pursuing their heart's passion and are committed to loosening the chains of injustice and setting the oppressed free, as the prophet Isaiah described (Isaiah 58:6). In their lives, significance—not merely personal success—reigns, and God is being glorified.

Exploring Possibilities, Part 2 (6 minutes)

This video segment explores the ways in which three people are responding to the challenges and possibilities of halftime.

- Despite her success in founding a CPA firm, Lillian Barger was missing something in her life. So she set a limit on the hours she would work and began speaking to trendsetting women about Jesus Christ.
- A successful businessman, Bill Simon seemingly had everything he had ever wanted, but it wasn't enough. One day he found himself divorced and realized that he wasn't as smart as he thought he was. Bill doesn't have everything figured out yet; that's what halftime is for. But he has realized that earthly success, by itself, doesn't have the sustaining power to complete his life. "You know," he says, "I feel that I'm in training to do God's will."
- Margaret Dye reared her children during the first half of her life. Then, as she put it, "Halftime for me was a time that I felt God was really calling me to slow down, stop, listen, and understand who I was as God designed me to be." Although she had planned to attend graduate school after her sons left for college, God guided her in a different direction. Today she is in a graduate school of a different type—serving as the local missions coordinator for her church.

All three of these people dared to open the window and dream a little. They chose to look beyond themselves and see what kind of adventure their second half could be.

Key Points of This Session

1. Halftime gives people in midlife the opportunity to explore possibilities, to realize that they can give themselves permission to dream about making changes, to look for ways in which they can discover and live out their calling based on who God created them to be.

2. Halftime is a time to slow down, listen to God, and be open to the implications of what he reveals. Often, to listen to God, people need

to take time out from the hustle and bustle of daily existence and find that place where the quiet voice of God is most audible.

3. Halftime isn't about getting away from it all. It's about a change of heart that urges people to move beyond their personal concerns and to ask the challenging questions that will lead them on a journey toward significance. It's a time for dedication to something much bigger than themselves so they can fulfill God's special calling for their lives.

Session Outline (56 minutes)

   I. **Introduction** (4 minutes)
   Welcome
   What's to Come
   Questions to Think About

   II. **Video Presentation, Part 1: "Exploring Possibilities"** (12 minutes)

   III. **Group Discovery** (15 minutes)
   Video Highlights (3 minutes)
   Large Group Exploration (6 minutes)
   Pause for Personal Reflection
   Small Group Exploration (6 minutes)
   Pause for Personal Reflection

   IV. **Video Presentation, Part 2: "Exploring Possibilities"** (7 minutes)

   V. **Group Discovery** (13 minutes)
   Video Highlights (3 minutes)
   Personal Exploration (5 minutes)
   Group Discussion (5 minutes)

   VI. **Action Points** (4 minutes)

   VII. **Closing Meditation** (1 minute)

Materials

You'll need a VCR, a television set, and a Bible, but no additional materials. Simply view both video segments prior to leading the session so you are familiar with the main points.

2

Exploring Possibilities

Beware the urge to get away from it all. That is not what the second half is all about. I know people who are well into their second halves who are still working at the same job they started with and who will be there to get the gold watch. The key to a successful second half is not a change of jobs; it is a change of heart—a change in the way you view the world and order your life.

Bob Buford

INTRODUCTION

4 minutes

Welcome

> Call the participants together. Welcome them to *Halftime* session 2, "Exploring Possibilities."

What's to Come

Regardless of where we live, how much money we make, what kind of talents we have, or even the mistakes we have made, all of us can explore new possibilities for our lives. During halftime, we can give ourselves permission to ask challenging questions and make changes that will lead toward significance.

We'll see two video presentations during this session. The first focuses on the fact that each of us has a God-given calling that guides us toward who he created us to be and what he created us to do. In light of that calling, each of us can choose whether, as Bob Buford puts it, to "give himself or herself over to something larger" than our personal concerns. We'll meet Bob and Tina Muzikowski, who have taken that step and chosen to become personally involved in reaching Chicago's inner-city youth.

In the second video segment, we'll see how three people—Lillian Barger, a successful CPA; Bill Simon, a businessman; and Margaret

Session

2

Exploring Possibilities

Beware the urge to get away from it all. That is not what the second half is all about. I know people who are well into their second halves who are still working at the same job they started with and who will be there to get the gold watch. The key to a successful second half is not a change of jobs; it is a change of heart—a change in the way you view the world and order your life.

Bob Buford

51

PLANNING NOTES

Dye, a former at-home mom whose children grew up and left home—are applying halftime principles to discover who God created them to be and undertake the adventure of living out their calling.

Questions to Think About

> **Have participants open their Participant's Guide to page 52.**
>
> **As time permits, ask two or more of the following questions and solicit responses from the participants.**

Let's begin this session by considering a few questions.

 1. Sometimes what we say we believe appears to be quite different from the way we actually live and the choices we make. In what ways have you found this to be true in your life and the lives of other people?

   Possible Answers: We may talk about values we hold dear, but it's much harder to make the sacrifices required to actually apply those values in daily life. Allow participants to share their personal experiences—the personal challenges they face when they seek to live according to what they believe. These may include not having the time or energy to make the necessary sacrifice, being afraid to put their faith on the line, being unwilling to upset the status quo or take financial risks, etc.

 2. How important is it to become personally involved in causes we really believe in? Why?

   Possible Answers: These may vary, but generally most participants will recognize that personal involvement moves us from a spectator mentality to a participant mode in which we actually participate in the game. When we jump in and do something significant, we begin to view our lives differently. We become participants in our own epic—a grand, ambitious journey that leads toward significance.

 3. What do you think a person needs to do to start thinking beyond what is and begin dreaming about what could be? What enables a person to explore the possibilities and view life as an epic—a grand, ambitious journey that leads toward significance?

   Possible Answers: Encourage participants to explore their personal requirements for pursuing a significant life. Responses will vary. Some individuals need to realize that they can make changes. Others need to realistically evaluate their strengths and weaknesses, goals and dreams. Others need to avoid comparing what they have accomplished so far to everybody else's achievements. Others need to examine their real motivations, be willing to change direction as needed, and realize that each of us can explore possi-

QUESTIONS TO THINK ABOUT

1. Sometimes what we say we believe appears to be quite different from the way we actually live and the choices we make. In what ways have you found this to be true in your life and the lives of other people?

2. How important is it to become personally involved in causes we really believe in? Why?

3. What do you think a person needs to do to start thinking beyond what is and begin dreaming about what could be? What enables a person to explore the possibilities and view life as an epic—a grand, ambitious journey that leads toward significance?

PLANNING NOTES

bilities no matter how much or little we have accomplished thus far. Some will need to talk with other people and discover how they could make a difference in people's lives.

Let's keep these ideas in mind as we view the first video segment. There is space in your Participant's Guide for taking notes.

VIDEO PRESENTATION, PART 1: "Exploring Possibilities"

Leader's Video Observations
Being a hero

minutes

Bob and Tina Muzikowski—choosing significance

Personal involvement

Personal sacrifice

Halftime—a change of heart

VIDEO NOTES, PART 1

Being a hero

Bob and Tina Muzikowski—choosing significance

Personal involvement

Personal sacrifice

Halftime—a change of heart

PLANNING NOTES

GROUP DISCOVERY

minutes

> If your group has seven or more members, use the **Video Highlights** (3 minutes) with the entire group, then complete the **Large Group Exploration** (6 minutes), then break into small groups of three to five people for the **Small Group Exploration** (6 minutes).
>
> If your group has fewer than seven members, begin with the **Video Highlights** (3 minutes), then complete both the **Large Group Exploration** (6 minutes) and the **Small Group Exploration** (6 minutes) as a group.

Video Highlights (3 minutes)

> As time permits, ask one or more of the following questions that directly relate to the video segment the participants have just seen.

Let's take a few moments to consider how Bob and Tina Muzikowski's halftime choices may relate to our lives.

 1. What do you think of the life Bob and Tina have chosen to pursue?

Possible Answers: These will vary. The most important thing is to encourage participants to honestly share their responses to the choices and lifestyle they saw portrayed through the video.

 2. Do you long to experience the passion and purpose in life that Bob and Tina seem to have? Describe what that passion and purpose might look like in your life.

Possible Answers: These will vary. Encourage participants to begin describing what a life of passion and purpose—a significant life—might look like to them.

 3. In what ways does Bob and Tina's response to the halftime process challenge you to evaluate your life and potential journey toward significance?

Possible Answers: Encourage participants to make a connection between Bob and Tina's choices and their own lives. Some participants may have realized that they too could cut back their working hours to pursue specific goals and still have the financial support they need. Others may have realized that they have long had a latent desire to make significant lifestyle changes that better represent their core beliefs. Others may have been challenged to think about how they might be able to do something significant, how easy it is to remain in a comfortable rut, how important it is for them (as a couple) to think about their calling at this point in life.

54　　　HALFTIME PARTICIPANT'S GUIDE

VIDEO HIGHLIGHTS

1. What do you think of the life Bob and Tina have chosen to pursue?

2. Do you long to experience the passion and purpose in life that Bob and Tina seem to have? Describe what that passion and purpose might look like in your life.

3. In what ways does Bob and Tina's response to the halftime process challenge you to evaluate your life and potential journey toward significance?

4. As you watched this video segment, what ideas came to mind regarding what you could do during your second half?

PLANNING NOTES

4. As you watched this video segment, what ideas came to mind regarding what you could do during your second half?

Possible Answers: Encourage participants to share their fledgling dreams with the group.

Large Group Exploration (6 minutes)

Pursuing Something Larger Than Our Personal Concerns

A hero is someone who gives himself or herself over to something larger than his or her personal concerns. In the Bible we find many stories of heroes—men and women who accepted the calling, the destiny, that God had for them. These men and women made the personal sacrifices necessary to pursue their unique calling, even when it led into previously uncharted territory. Let's read about a few of these heroes of the Bible and see what we learn about how they each recognized their calling and responded to it.

 1. Abram (whose name was later changed to Abraham)—Genesis 12:1–5

Possible Answer: God called Abram to leave his country and extended family and go to the land God would show him. God also promised to make him the father of a great nation, to bless him, and to make him a blessing to others. So at age seventy-five Abram obeyed God. Taking his wife, family, and possessions, he set out for a new land.

 2. Moses—Exodus 3:1–4, 7–12; 4:20 (If time permits, see 3:13–4:19 also.)

Possible Answer: Moses was going about his shepherding business when he saw something unusual (a burning bush) and went to investigate. God then spoke to Moses, revealing his plan and the role he had chosen Moses to play in that plan. After wrestling with God regarding his doubts, Moses did what he was called to do and led the Hebrew nation out of Egypt.

 3. Mordecai's adopted daughter, Esther, the Jewish woman who became the wife of King Xerxes of Persia—Esther 2:17–20; 3:8–11; 4:1, 5–16

Possible Answer: Mordecai urged Esther to go before the king and plead for the lives of the Jewish people. At first she refused because it could cost her her life. Mordecai then pointed out that this could be her God-given calling. Recognizing that truth, she agreed to approach the king, even if it meant her death, and became the instrument by which God saved his people.

 4. Paul—Acts 9:1–6, 10–22

VIDEO HIGHLIGHTS

1. What do you think of the life Bob and Tina have chosen to pursue?

2. Do you long to experience the passion and purpose in life that Bob and Tina seem to have? Describe what that passion and purpose might look like in your life.

3. In what ways does Bob and Tina's response to the halftime process challenge you to evaluate your life and potential journey toward significance?

4. As you watched this video segment, what ideas came to mind regarding what you could do during your second half?

PLANNING NOTES

LARGE GROUP EXPLORATION

Pursuing Something Larger Than Our Personal Concerns

A hero is someone who gives himself or herself over to something larger than his or her personal concerns. In the Bible we find many stories of heroes—men and women who accepted the calling, the destiny, that God had for them. These men and women made the personal sacrifices necessary to pursue their unique calling, even when it led into previously uncharted territory. Let's read about a few of these heroes of the Bible and see what we learn about how they each recognized their calling and responded to it.

1. Abram (whose name was later changed to Abraham)—Genesis 12:1–5.

2. Moses—Exodus 3:1–4, 7–12; 4:20 (If time permits, see 3:13–4:19 also.)

---

3. Mordecai's adopted daughter, Esther, the Jewish woman who became the wife of King Xerxes of Persia—Esther 2:17–20; 3:8–11; 4:1, 5–16

4. Paul—Acts 9:1–6, 10–22

5. Daniel—Daniel 6:6–27

Pause for Personal Reflection

Now it's time to pause to consider God's calling for each of us and the ways in which he might be revealing it.

Do I believe that God has a calling—a specific purpose—for everyone? If so, how important is it for me to discover and pursue my calling?

Possible Answer: Paul was eagerly persecuting Christians when Jesus stopped him in his tracks and temporarily blinded him. Jesus told Paul to go to Damascus and wait for instructions. As Paul waited, Jesus told Ananias to go to Paul and restore his sight because God had chosen Paul to carry his message to many people. Neither of these men would ever have guessed what God would call them to do, but they each obeyed. The result was that Paul astonished people by fulfilling his calling and preaching about Jesus.

 5. Daniel—Daniel 6:6–27

Possible Answer: After King Darius of Babylon decreed that his people could pray only to him, Daniel continued to be faithful to God and to pray to God as he always had done. As punishment, Daniel was thrown into the lions' den, but he did not die. His faithful obedience to God resulted in King Darius praising the living God and requiring his people to do the same.

Pause for Personal Reflection

Now it's time to pause to consider God's calling for each of us and the ways in which he might be revealing it.

- Do I believe that God has a calling—a specific purpose—for everyone? If so, how important is it for me to discover and pursue my calling?
- Have I taken God's calling for my life into account when I have made significant plans in the past? Why or why not?
- In what ways might God be revealing his calling for me? What do I think that calling might be?

Let participants know when there is one minute remaining.

3. Mordecai's adopted daughter, Esther, the Jewish woman who became the wife of King Xerxes of Persia—Esther 2:17–20; 3:8–11; 4:1, 5–16

4. Paul—Acts 9:1–6, 10–22

5. Daniel—Daniel 6:6–27

Pause for Personal Reflection

Now it's time to pause to consider God's calling for each of us and the ways in which he might be revealing it.

Do I believe that God has a calling—a specific purpose—for everyone? If so, how important is it for me to discover and pursue my calling?

Have I taken God's calling for my life into account when I have made significant plans in the past? Why or why not?

In what ways might God be revealing his calling for me? What do I think that calling might be?

HALFTIME DRILL

Leading Questions for Exploring Your Calling

In his book *Halftime,* Bob Buford reminds us that "halftime is more than putting your feet up and meditating. It's more than time away to think, pray, and play. A successful halftime needs some structure. Set an agenda that will help you 'walk' through the important issues. Such an agenda will indeed include time to pray and listen, to read the Scriptures, and to think, but it should also include some deliberate questions."

The following questions may guide you as you begin to explore what your God-given calling may be.

1. What is my passion?

2. Where do I belong?

3. What do I believe? And what will I do about what I believe?

4. How am I wired?

Continued on next page...

PLANNING NOTES

Leading Questions for Exploring Your Calling

In his book *Halftime,* Bob Buford reminds us that "halftime is more than putting your feet up and meditating. It's more than time away to think, pray, and play. A successful halftime needs some structure. Set an agenda that will help you 'walk' through the important issues. Such an agenda will indeed include time to pray and listen, to read the Scriptures, and to think, but it should also include some deliberate questions."

The following questions may guide you as you begin to explore what your God-given calling may be.

1. What is my passion?

2. Where do I belong?

3. What do I believe? And what will I do about what I believe?

4. How am I wired?

5. What are my core values? And to what degree should I make key decisions based on these values?

6. What are my aspirations?

7. What do I have to do, learn, and/or change to become capable of living up to the demands I place on myself and to fulfill my expectations of life?

8. For what regrets or mistakes do I need to forgive myself—and to view as markers from which I can learn valuable lessons?

9. What do I want to be doing in ten years? In twenty years?

10. What gifts has God given me that have been perfected over time? What gifts has God given me that I'm unable to use?

11. What changes might I need to make to better align my job and career with my true self?

12. If I remain on the same track, pursuing the same types of things I am pursuing today, where will I end up?

Have I taken God's calling for my life into account when I have made significant plans in the past? Why or why not?

In what ways might God be revealing his calling for me? What do I think that calling might be?

HALFTIME DRILL

Leading Questions for Exploring Your Calling

In his book *Halftime,* Bob Buford reminds us that "halftime is more than putting your feet up and meditating. It's more than time away to think, pray, and play. A successful halftime needs some structure. Set an agenda that will help you 'walk' through the important issues. Such an agenda will indeed include time to pray and listen, to read the Scriptures, and to think, but it should also include some deliberate questions."

The following questions may guide you as you begin to explore what your God-given calling may be.

1. What is my passion?

2. Where do I belong?

3. What do I believe? And what will I do about what I believe?

4. How am I wired?

Continued on next page...

5. What are my core values? And to what degree should I make key decisions based on these values?

6. What are my aspirations?

7. What do I have to do, learn, and/or change to become capable of living up to the demands I place on myself and to fulfill my expectations of life?

8. For what regrets or mistakes do I need to forgive myself — and view as markers from which I can learn valuable lessons?

9. What do I want to be doing in ten years? In twenty years?

10. What gifts has God given me that have been perfected over time? What gifts has God given me that I'm unable to use?

11. What changes might I need to make in order to better align my job and career with my true self?

12. If I remain on the same track, pursuing the same types of things I am pursuing today, where will I end up?

PLANNING NOTES

Small Group Exploration (6 minutes)

Needed: A Change of Heart

In the video segment, Bob Buford said, "The key to a successful second half is not a change of jobs. It's a change of heart." Let's take a few minutes to consider what kind of change of heart leads to a significant second half.

 1. The changes Bob and Tina Muzikowski made in their lives sprang out of a change of heart. Bob cut back on his hours as a benefits planner and agent for Northwestern Mutual and earns less than he used to. To be a part of the community they felt led to serve, they moved from the suburbs and into the city. In light of these changes and the challenges they have encountered, why was the change of heart he and Tina experienced so important?

Possible Answer: If Bob and Tina had made these dramatic lifestyle changes without a corresponding change of heart, they could easily have become discouraged when they moved away from their friends, when they made personal sacrifices because of their reduced income, when the boy whose bicycle they fixed up was killed. To do what they did (and are doing), they needed a change of heart and sense of purpose greater than themselves.

 2. In the Bible, the word *heart* is used to describe the deepest part of a person—the core of his or her being. Read each of the following verses and note what they teach us about the human heart and what brings about a change of heart.

Scripture	The Truth About the Human Heart
Matthew 6:19–21	*What we accumulate as treasure reveals the focus of our heart.*
Matthew 22:37–40 (also Deut. 6:5–6)	*We are to love the Lord our God with all our heart, soul, mind, and strength. This commandment is at the core of all other commandments, thus it is to be at the core of our behavior as well.*
Hebrews 4:12	*The Word of God, which is "living and active," penetrates the deepest parts of our being, judging the thoughts and attitudes of our hearts. Thus the work of the Word of God is the basis for a change of heart.*
Hebrews 4:13	*We are accountable to God for what is in our hearts.*
Jeremiah 17:10	*God searches our hearts, examines our minds, and will reward us according to our deeds and conduct.*
Proverbs 21:2	*We can do things that seem right to us, but God weighs our hearts—what's at the deepest core of our being.*

SMALL GROUP EXPLORATION

Needed: A Change of Heart

In the video segment, Bob Buford said, "The key to a successful second half is not a change of jobs. It's a change of heart." Let's take a few minutes to consider what kind of change of heart leads to a significant second half.

1. The changes Bob and Tina Muzikowski made in their lives sprang out of a change of heart. Bob cut back on his hours as a benefits planner and agent for Northwestern Mutual and earns less than he used to. To be a part of the community they felt led to serve, they moved from the suburbs and into the city. In light of these changes and the challenges they have encountered, why was the change of heart he and Tina experienced so important?

2. In the Bible, the word *heart* is used to describe the deepest part of a person—the core of his or her being. Read each of the following verses and note what they teach us about the human heart and what brings about a change of heart.

Scripture	The Truth About the Human Heart
Matthew 6:19–21	
Matthew 22:37–40 (also Deut. 6:5–6)	

Continued on next page...

Scripture	The Truth About the Human Heart
Hebrews 4:12	
Hebrews 4:13	
Jeremiah 17:10	
Proverbs 21:2	

Pause for Personal Reflection

Now it's time to pause to consider where our hearts are focused.

As I read the verses describing the human heart, what did I discover about my heart?

What is the true focus of my heart?

PLANNING NOTES

Pause for Personal Reflection

Now it's time to pause to consider where our hearts are focused.

- As I read the verses describing the human heart, what did I discover about my heart?
- What is the true focus of my heart?
- Which aspects of my life—my thoughts, my words, my actions—fall into place according to that focus?

> **Let participants know when there is one minute remaining.**

VIDEO PRESENTATION, PART 2: "Exploring Possibilities"

minutes

> **Transition participants into part 2 of this session.**

Now that we've discussed some topics related to part 1 of this session, let's view the second video segment.

Leader's Video Observations

Lillian Barger—exploring a parallel career

Bill Simon—in training to do God's will

Margaret Dye—listening for God's purpose

Scripture	The Truth About the Human Heart
Hebrews 4:12	
Hebrews 4:13	
Jeremiah 17:10	
Proverbs 21:2	

Pause for Personal Reflection

Now it's time to pause to consider where our hearts are focused.

As I read the verses describing the human heart, what did I discover about my heart?

What is the true focus of my heart?

Which aspects of my life—my thoughts, my words, my actions—fall into place according to that focus?

VIDEO NOTES, PART 2

Lillian Barger—exploring a parallel career

Bill Simon—in training to do God's will

Margaret Dye—listening for God's purpose

PLANNING NOTES

GROUP DISCOVERY

minutes

> Use the **Video Highlights** (3 minutes) with the entire group, then allow participants to complete the **Personal Exploration** (5 minutes), then do the **Group Discussion** (5 minutes), which includes questions from both parts 1 and 2.

Video Highlights (3 minutes)

> As time permits, ask one or more of the following questions that directly relate to the video segment the participants have just seen.

 1. In what ways did you identify with Lillian, Bill, and Margaret as they talked about their halftime explorations and discoveries? What impact did their experiences have on you?

Possible Answers: Encourage participants to share about what touched or inspired them as they listened to these people share their experiences. Responses may include being excited about how God might use me, wondering if this is the right time to begin exploring halftime concerns, considering what it will take to discover my God-given destiny, realizing that what I've built my life on so far isn't all there is, wanting the rest of my life to be better, wanting to get out of my rut, etc.

 2. Rena Pederson observed that the halftime process is often different for women than it is for men. In what ways might halftime be different? In what ways might it be similar?

Possible Answers: Halftime is not a cookie-cutter process. Encourage participants to realize that halftime isn't just for forty-plus-year-old white males who make six-figure incomes. It is also for women who have chosen to be homemakers and, after their children have left home, ask, "What's next?" It is for men and women who have had successful careers and realize that "something is missing, there's more to life than I now have." It is for men and women who say, "I've done this all of my life; what can I do that better represents who God made me to be?"

42   HALFTIME PARTICIPANT'S GUIDE

VIDEO HIGHLIGHTS

1. In what ways did you identify with Lillian, Bill, and Margaret as they talked about their halftime explorations and discoveries? What impact did their experiences have on you?

2. Rena Pederson observed that the halftime process is often different for women than it is for men. In what ways might halftime be different? In what ways might it be similar?

HALFTIME CLIP

Some people make the mistake of using halftime to fantasize, wistfully projecting various images of themselves into unrealistic situations that will never happen. But getting ready for a better second half is not daydreaming. You need to honestly face the tough, nitty-gritty questions about finances, other family members, and long-range goals. And when you do ask the hard questions, don't fudge on the answers. To make the second half better than the first, you need to discover the real you. **—BOB BUFORD**

PLANNING NOTES

HALFTIME CLIP

Some people make the mistake of using halftime to fantasize, wistfully projecting various images of themselves into unrealistic situations that will never happen. But getting ready for a better second half is not daydreaming. You need to honestly face the tough, nittygritty questions about finances, other family members, and long-range goals. And when you do ask the hard questions, don't fudge on the answers. To make the second half better than the first, you need to discover the real you.

—BOB BUFORD

Personal Exploration (5 minutes)

Barriers That Hold Us Back

Regardless of where we live, how much money we make, what talents we have, and even the mistakes we have made, we can give ourselves permission to be open to new possibilities that lead toward significance. Yet many of us find it difficult to actually live as if new possibilities are available to us. We may have lots to say when we're asked what we're missing in our lives, what we value, or what we might like to be doing in five to ten years, but we fail to set aside the time and energy to reflect on these possibilities and pursue them.

1. Consider the following common attitudes and beliefs that can negatively impact our ability to dream about new opportunities and pursue a significant second half. Check off the barriers that are most challenging to you and note the impact they have had on your life.

   ❑ I am overly influenced by other people's (or society's) expectations of who I should be. As a result, I _____
   _____.

   ❑ Financial concerns are very important to me. I have too little money (or too much money to put at risk) to cut back on my schedule and pursue some dream that I hope will lead to significance. As a result, I _____
   _____.

   ❑ I like knowing what's ahead, so I stay on the present course. I don't like the uncertainty and fear that come when I start thinking about different opportunities for the future. It's too confusing. As a result, I _____.

42   HALFTIME PARTICIPANT'S GUIDE

VIDEO HIGHLIGHTS

1. In what ways did you identify with Lillian, Bill, and Margaret as they talked about their halftime explorations and discoveries? What impact did their experiences have on you?

2. Rena Pederson observed that the halftime process is often different for women than it is for men. In what ways might halftime be different? In what ways might it be similar?

HALFTIME CLIP

Some people make the mistake of using halftime to fantasize, wistfully projecting various images of themselves into unrealistic situations that will never happen. But getting ready for a better second half is not daydreaming. You need to honestly face the tough, nitty-gritty questions about finances, other family members, and long-range goals. And when you do ask the hard questions, don't fudge on the answers. To make the second half better than the first, you need to discover the real you. —**BOB BUFORD**

PLANNING NOTES

SESSION TWO: Exploring Possibilities   **43**

PERSONAL EXPLORATION

Barriers That Hold Us Back

Regardless of where we live, how much money we make, what talents we have, and even the mistakes we have made, we can give ourselves permission to be open to new possibilities that lead toward significance. Yet many of us find it difficult to actually live as if new possibilities are available to us. We may have lots to say when we're asked what we're missing in our lives, what we value, or what we might like to be doing in five to ten years, but we fail to set aside the time and energy to reflect on these possibilities and pursue them.

1. Consider the following common attitudes and beliefs that can negatively impact our ability to dream about new opportunities and pursue a significant second half. Check off the barriers that are most challenging to you and note the impact they have had on your life.

   ❑ I am overly influenced by other people's (or society's) expectations of who I should be. As a result, I _____
   _____.

   ❑ Financial concerns are very important to me. I have too little money (or too much money to put at risk) to cut back on my schedule and pursue some dream that I hope will lead to significance. As a result, I _____
   _____.

---

44   HALFTIME PARTICIPANT'S GUIDE

   ❑ I like knowing what's ahead, so I stay on the present course. I don't like the uncertainty and fear that come when I start thinking about different opportunities for the future. It's too confusing. As a result, I _____
   _____.

   ❑ I have so much to do today that I can't take time out to think about future possibilities. Thinking about the future doesn't accomplish anything for me today. As a result, I
   _____
   _____.

   ❑ I've been successful, but I've failed God and hurt other people in the process. I'm not so sure I deserve a better second half. As a result, I _____.

   ❑ God might have something for me to do, but I can't see my gifts, talents, knowledge, experiences, or training leading to anything big, exciting, or significant. As a result, I
   _____
   _____.

❏ I have so much to do today that I can't take time out to think about future possibilities. Thinking about the future doesn't accomplish anything for me today. As a result, I _____ _____.

❏ I've been successful, but I've failed God and hurt other people in the process. I'm not so sure I deserve a better second half. As a result, I _____.

❏ God might have something for me to do, but I can't see my gifts, talents, knowledge, experiences, or training leading to anything big, exciting, or significant. As a result, I _____ _____.

❏ When I no longer have what it takes to stay on top of my game, I'll be miserable. Life will be downhill from that point on. As a result, I _____.

❏ I'd like to do something significant, but not if I'm going to lose any of the power and prestige I enjoy today. As a result, I _____ _____.

❏ I'd like to do something significant, and I have several areas of interest, but there's nothing compelling that I feel led io pursue. As a result, I _____.

2. Write down any additional barriers that are keeping you from exploring the opportunity to discover a significant second half.

3. For each barrier you checked, write down specific actions you could take to begin facing and overcoming that barrier.

4. What will be the consequences if you do not deal with these barriers soon?

HALFTIME CLIP

For me, the transition into the afternoon of life was a time for reordering my time and my treasure, for reconfiguring my values and my vision of what life could be. It represented more than a renewal; it was a new beginning. It was more than a reality check; it was a fresh and leisurely look into the holiest chamber of my own heart, affording me, at last, an opportunity to respond to my soul's deepest longings. **—BOB BUFORD**

❏ I like knowing what's ahead, so I stay on the present course. I don't like the uncertainty and fear that come when I start thinking about different opportunities for the future. It's too confusing. As a result, I _____

_____.

❏ I have so much to do today that I can't take time out to think about future possibilities. Thinking about the future doesn't accomplish anything for me today. As a result, I

_____

_____.

❏ I've been successful, but I've failed God and hurt other people in the process. I'm not so sure I deserve a better second half. As a result, I _____.

_____

❏ God might have something for me to do, but I can't see my gifts, talents, knowledge, experiences, or training leading to anything big, exciting, or significant. As a result, I

_____

_____.

PLANNING NOTES

_____

_____

_____

_____

_____

_____

_____

_____

_____

_____

_____

_____

_____

_____

_____

❏ When I no longer have what it takes to stay on top of my game, I'll be miserable. Life will be downhill from that point on. As a result, I _____

_____.

❏ I'd like to do something significant, but not if I'm going to lose any of the power and prestige I enjoy today. As a result, I _____

_____.

❏ I'd like to do something significant, and I have several areas of interest, but there's nothing compelling that I feel led to pursue. As a result, I _____

_____.

2. Write down any additional barriers that are keeping you from exploring the opportunity to discover a significant second half.

3. For each barrier you checked, write down specific actions you could take to begin facing and overcoming that barrier.

4. What will be the consequences if you do not deal with these barriers soon?

HALFTIME CLIP

For me, the transition into the afternoon of life was a time for reordering my time and my treasure, for reconfiguring my values and my vision of what life could be. It represented more than a renewal; it was a new beginning. It was more than a reality check; it was a fresh and leisurely look into the holiest chamber of my own heart, affording me, at last, an opportunity to respond to my soul's deepest longings.
—BOB BUFORD

A Hope for the Future

The halftime process is certainly challenging and at times even frightening. Yet when we seek to know God and to follow his leading in life, we can explore the possibilities and approach the uncertainties of halftime with hope and confidence because God promises to be with us. Notice the following promises and take heart as you explore new possibilities for the second half of your life!

God's Promises	Scripture
God is with us always, offering guidance and counsel as he leads us to our ultimate destination.	Psalm 73:23–24
God is attentive to the prayers of righteous people who believe in him.	1 Peter 3:12
We don't need to chase after the necessities of life. God, who believes each of us is valuable, will care for and meet the needs of those who seek his kingdom and his righteousness above all else.	Matthew 6:25–26; 31–33
We can hold on to our hope with confidence because God will remain faithful to his promises no matter what.	Hebrews 10:23
God has plans for his people—plans for their benefit that give them a hope and a future.	Jeremiah 29:11
God has created his people to do good works that he prepares in advance for them to do.	Ephesians 2:10
God is our refuge and strength, always available to help us.	Psalm 46:1

Let participants know when there is one minute remaining.

HALFTIME PERSPECTIVE

A Hope for the Future

The halftime process is certainly challenging and at times even frightening. Yet when we seek to know God and to follow his leading in life, we can explore the possibilities and approach the uncertainties of halftime with hope and confidence because God promises to be with us. Notice the following promises and take heart as you explore new possibilities for the second half of your life!

God's Promises	Scripture
God is with us always, offering guidance and counsel as he leads us to our ultimate destination.	Psalm 73:23–24
God is attentive to the prayers of righteous people who believe in him.	1 Peter 3:12
We don't need to chase after the necessities of life. God, who believes each of us is valuable, will care for and meet the needs of those who seek his kingdom and his righteousness above all else.	Matthew 6:25–26; 31–33
We can hold on to our hope with confidence because God will remain faithful to his promises no matter what.	Hebrews 10:23
God has plans for his people—plans for their benefit that give them a hope and a future.	Jeremiah 29:11
God has created his people to do good works that he prepares in advance for them to do.	Ephesians 2:10
God is our refuge and strength, always available to help us.	Psalm 46:1

PLANNING NOTES

Group Discussion (5 minutes)

Now it's time to wrap up our discovery time.

> Give participants a moment to transition from their thoughtfulness and begin sharing their observations with the entire group. Use the following questions as discussion starters.

 1. Now that you've seen some people who are discovering their callings and committing themselves to doing something significant during the second half of life, something that wells up from deep within themselves, what do you find yourself thinking about or feeling? Do you feel sad about what you haven't done? Have you been inspired to start thinking in new directions? To do something?

 2. What did you discover about the process of making significant changes in life as you listened to the experiences of people you saw in the video segment?

 3. Let's review some of the reasons why people who are in or are approaching halftime should evaluate the possibilities that can lead to a significant second half.

 4. What are the differences in attitude, lifestyle, and future benefits between simply doing something you enjoy and giving yourself over to something larger than your personal concerns?

 5. In light of what we've learned during this session, why is it important to take time to listen to God and be open to the implications of what he reveals as we explore our dreams and desires during the halftime process?

HALFTIME TIP

> Which transition options below best fit your temperament and gifts?
> - Keep doing what you are doing, but change the environment.
> - Change what you are doing, but stay in the same environment.
> - Turn an avocation into a career.
> - Double-track (or even triple-track) in parallel careers (not hobbies).
> - Keep doing what you are doing, even past retirement age.

GROUP DISCUSSION

1. Now that you've seen some people who are discovering their callings and committing themselves to doing something significant during the second half of life, something that wells up from deep within themselves, what do you find yourself thinking about or feeling? Do you feel sad about what you haven't done? Have you been inspired to start thinking in new directions? To do something?

2. What did you discover about the process of making significant changes in life as you listened to the experiences of people you saw in the video segment?

3. Let's review some of the reasons why people who are in or are approaching halftime should evaluate the possibilities that can lead to a significant second half.

4. What are the differences in attitude, lifestyle, and future benefits between simply doing something you enjoy and giving yourself over to something larger than your personal concerns?

5. In light of what we've learned during this session, why is it important to take time to listen to God and be open to the implications of what he reveals as we explore our dreams and desires during the halftime process?

HALFTIME TIP

Which transition options below best fit your temperament and gifts?

- Keep doing what you are doing, but change the environment.
- Change what you are doing, but stay in the same environment.
- Turn an avocation into a career.
- Double-track (or even triple-track) in parallel careers (not hobbies).
- Keep doing what you are doing, even past retirement age.

PLANNING NOTES

ACTION POINTS

minutes

> **The following points are reproduced on page 50 of the Participant's Guide.**

I'd like to take a moment to summarize the key points we explored today. After I have reviewed these points, I will give you a moment to consider what you will commit to do as a result of what you have discovered during this session.

> **Read the following points and pause afterward so participants can consider and write out their commitments.**

 1. Halftime gives people in midlife the opportunity to explore possibilities, to realize that they can give themselves permission to dream about making changes, to look for ways in which they can discover and live out their calling based on who God created them to be.

   What steps are you willing to take to begin discovering the calling God has for your life? These steps may be as varied as "talking to my spouse about certain possibilities," "taking a class on _____," "taking a weekend away from everything just to think and dream," "volunteering at _____ for _____," or "reading that book I've always wanted to read."

   Write down these steps!

 2. Halftime is a time to slow down, listen to God, and be open to the implications of what he reveals. Often, to listen to God, people need to take time out from the hustle and bustle of daily existence and find that place where the quiet voice of God is most audible.

   What changes will you make in your routine that will give you more time to slow down and listen to God—and to your own dreams and desires for the future?

   What is the best way for you to structure that time with God?

   If nothing else, set aside at least one hour this week during which, away from most or all distractions, you can begin thinking about your halftime possibilities and listening for God's leading.

ACTION POINTS

What will you commit to do as a result of what you have discovered during this session?

1. Halftime gives people in midlife the opportunity to explore possibilities, to realize that they can give themselves permission to dream about making changes, to look for ways in which they can discover and live out their calling based on who God created them to be.

   What steps are you willing to take to begin discovering the calling God has for your life? These steps may be as varied as "talking to my spouse about certain possibilities," "taking a class on _____," "taking a weekend away from everything just to think and dream," "volunteering at _____ for _____," or "reading that book I've always wanted to read."

   Write down these steps!

2. Halftime is a time to slow down, listen to God, and be open to the implications of what he reveals. Often, to listen to God, people need to take time out from the hustle and bustle of daily existence and find that place where the quiet voice of God is most audible.

What changes will you make in your routine that will give you more time to slow down and listen to God—and to your own dreams and desires for the future?

What is the best way for you to structure that time with God?

If nothing else, set aside at least one hour this week during which, away from most or all distractions, you can begin thinking about your halftime possibilities and listening for God's leading.

3. Halftime isn't about getting away from it all. It's about a change of heart that urges people to move beyond their personal concerns and to ask the challenging questions that will lead them on a journey toward significance. It's a time to dedicate themselves to something much bigger than themselves so they can fulfill God's special calling for their lives.

   How important is it to you to become involved in a cause much larger than your personal concerns? How would its importance change if you believed God was guiding you in that direction?

PLANNING NOTES

3. Halftime isn't about getting away from it all. It's about a change of heart that urges people to move beyond their personal concerns and to ask the challenging questions that will lead them on a journey toward significance. It's a time to dedicate themselves to something much bigger than themselves so they can fulfill God's special calling for their lives.

How important is it to you to become involved in a cause much larger than your personal concerns? How would its importance change if you believed God was guiding you in that direction?

On what is your heart focused right now? Do you need to ask God to change your heart and reveal the larger cause to which he may be calling you?

To the best of your ability at this point, describe the larger cause that might play a role in a significant second half for you.

HALFTIME CLIP

Don't expect to solve all your first-half issues and plan for the second half in a few hours. For most people, halftime takes several months, even years. But it will never happen if we don't give it the time it deserves.
—BOB BUFORD

CLOSING MEDITATION

minute

Dear God, it's not easy to begin evaluating the possibilities we can have during the second half of our lives. But it's also exciting to think about the calling you have for each of us that is truly much bigger than our personal concerns. Guide us as we discover and rediscover what it means to place our faith in you, and what it means to experience a change of heart. Most important, make us aware of how much you long for us to make more time to listen to you and study your Word. We need you, Lord. Teach us how to listen to you, and help us to be open to the implications of what you reveal to us. Amen.

What changes will you make in your routine that will give you more time to slow down and listen to God—and to your own dreams and desires for the future?

What is the best way for you to structure that time with God?

If nothing else, set aside at least one hour this week during which, away from most or all distractions, you can begin thinking about your halftime possibilities and listening for God's leading.

3. Halftime isn't about getting away from it all. It's about a change of heart that urges people to move beyond their personal concerns and to ask the challenging questions that will lead them on a journey toward significance. It's a time to dedicate themselves to something much bigger than themselves so they can fulfill God's special calling for their lives.

How important is it to you to become involved in a cause much larger than your personal concerns? How would its importance change if you believed God was guiding you in that direction?

On what is your heart focused right now? Do you need to ask God to change your heart and reveal the larger cause to which he may be calling you?

To the best of your ability at this point, describe the larger cause that might play a role in a significant second half for you.

HALFTIME CLIP

Don't expect to solve all your first-half issues and plan for the second half in a few hours. For most people, halftime takes several months, even years. But it will never happen if we don't give it the time it deserves.

—BOB BUFORD

PLANNING NOTES

Guidelines for a Successful Halftime

Many times, a good second half depends on what is done during halftime. The following concepts helped Bob Buford prepare to launch into the second half of his life.

1. *Make peace with your first-half issues.* This doesn't mean that you are proud of all you've done or that you would change nothing in your life if you could. Any honest look back will recall several things you wish you had done differently. The key is to keep these things in perspective and to accept them as an inevitable part of growth.

2. *Take time for the things that are really important.* This requires a certain amount of discipline and time management, and there will be the tendency to view this as yet another appointment on your already overscheduled date book. But you can take the time. Konosuke Matsushita, chairman of the huge and highly successful Japanese electronics company bearing his last name, follows the practice, not uncommon in Asia, of retreating to his garden from time to time to live a contemplative and reflective life. And when he walks into a room, the awe is palpable. Without saying a word, he bespeaks a powerful centeredness and elegant reserve.

3. *Be deliberate.* Halftime is more than putting your feet up and meditating. It's more than time away to think, pray, and play. A successful halftime needs structure. Set an agenda that will help you walk through the important issues.

4. *Share the journey.* Bob Buford cannot imagine making his transition from the first half to the second without being accompanied on the journey by his wife. She asked questions, made suggestions, kept him honest. If your marriage is truly a partnership, it would be wrong to impose a whole new lifestyle on your spouse without his or her input. If you are not married, seek out an accountability partner who will listen, encourage, and help keep you on track.

5. *Be honest.* Getting ready for a better second half is not daydreaming. You need to honestly face the tough, nitty-gritty questions about finances, other family members, and long-range goals. When you ask the hard questions, don't fudge on the answers. Your second half will focus on your true self, so be honest enough to discover it.

6. *Be patient.* It took you the better part of two decades or longer to reach this point. You can't undo everything overnight. You will still have to go to work tomorrow. Bills will arrive in the mail. Clients will expect to have their calls returned. And a clear picture of what you should do with the second half of your life may not emerge anytime soon.

7. *Have faith.* For Christians, halftime is basically a time to answer the question, "What will I do about what I believe?" Begin to answer that by putting your faith to work, by trusting God to guide you. Listen to his voice through Scripture and the thoughts he brings to mind as you talk with him.

HALFTIME PERSPECTIVE

Guidelines for a Successful Halftime

Many times, a good second half depends on what is done during halftime. The following concepts helped Bob Buford prepare to launch into the second half of his life.

1. Make peace with your first-half issues. This doesn't mean that you are proud of all you've done or that you would change nothing in your life if you could. Any honest look back will recall several things you wish you had done differently. The key is to keep these things in perspective and to accept them as an inevitable part of growth.

2. Take time for the things that are really important. This requires a certain amount of discipline and time management, and there will be the tendency to view this as yet another appointment on your already overscheduled date book. But you can take the time. Konosuke Matsushita, chairman of the huge and highly successful Japanese electronics company bearing his last name, follows the practice, not uncommon in Asia, of retreating to his garden from time to time to live a contemplative and reflective life. And when he walks into a room, the awe is palpable. Without saying a word, he bespeaks a powerful centeredness and elegant reserve.

3. Be deliberate. Halftime is more than putting your feet up and meditating. It's more than time away to think, pray, and play. A successful halftime needs structure. Set an agenda that will help you walk through the important issues.

4. Share the journey. Bob Buford cannot imagine making his transition from the first half to the second without being accompanied on the journey by his wife. She asked questions, made suggestions, kept him honest. If your marriage is truly a partnership, it would be wrong to impose a whole new lifestyle on your spouse without his or her input. If you are not married, seek out an accountability partner who will listen, encourage, and help keep you on track.

Continued on next page...

5. Be honest. Getting ready for a better second half is not daydreaming. You need to honestly face the tough, nitty-gritty questions about finances, other family members, and long-range goals. When you ask the hard questions, don't fudge on the answers. Your second half will focus on your true self, so be honest enough to discover it.

6. Be patient. It took you the better part of two decades or longer to reach this point. You can't undo everything overnight. You will still have to go to work tomorrow. Bills will arrive in the mail. Clients will expect to have their calls returned. And a clear picture of what you should do with the second half of your life may not emerge anytime soon.

7. Have faith. For Christians, halftime is basically a time to answer the question, "What will I do about what I believe?" Begin to answer that by putting your faith to work, by trusting God to guide you. Listen to his voice through Scripture and the thoughts he brings to mind as you talk with him.

PLANNING NOTES

3

What's in the Box?

BEFORE YOU LEAD

Synopsis

When Bob Buford reached a turning point during his early forties, he met with a strategic planner to sort out what he was going to do next. At one point in their discussions, the planner drew a box on a piece of paper and said, "I'm going to ask you what's in the box. For you, it is either money or Jesus Christ. If you can tell me which it is, I can tell you the strategic planning implications of that choice. If you can't tell me, you are going to oscillate between those two values and be confused for a lifetime."

That simple, penetrating question, "What's in the box?" challenged Bob to determine the one thing—the core value or belief, the primary loyalty, the overriding desire, the most essential part of himself—that would provide a sense of purpose and direction to motivate him for the second half of his life.

Likewise, the purpose of this session is to motivate each participant to determine the one thing he or she will put into the box for the second half of life. Each of us needs to draw up a strategic plan for ourselves, and that starts with choosing the one thing that will be in our box. Knowing what's in the box brings focus and clarity to the second half of life. The next step is to help each participant establish a solid foundation of beliefs from which his or her values, attitudes, and actions will flow.

In the video segment, you'll meet three people who discovered the one thing that made each of them tick: Karol Emmerich, who was the vice president, treasurer, and chief accounting officer of Dayton-Hudson Corporation; Jim Thweatt, who was a Wall Street stockbroker; and Bob Buford, who was chairman of the board and chief executive officer of Buford Television, Inc. They are living proof that making decisions based on "What's in the box?" leads to an exciting, significant second half.

As we saw in the previous video segment, some people choose to remain in their jobs and develop parallel careers. But Karol and Jim walked away from their careers—away from the dream life—and followed their dreams. Karol literally created a garden in which people from all over the country can come for a retreat. Jim is planting truth and values in the lives of inner-city youth.

This video segment also addresses the other side of halftime—the dark side. Sometimes a personal crisis causes people to ask, "What's in my box?" Tim Sambrano and Rogers Kirven are two businessmen who discovered they had all the money and freedom they'd dreamed of, yet weren't fulfilled. They, and others like them, didn't know which way to turn. They didn't have anything in the box to bring purpose and vitality to life. Lost and directionless, they were fortunate enough to realize their loss before their lives took a disastrous turn.

Bob Buford shares how important it is for us to trust God to lead and direct us not just during halftime but through all of life. After the sudden death of his son, Ross, Bob realized how quickly our earthly success can disappear. He thought, *This is a thing you can't buy your way out of, and you can't think your way out of, and you can't persuade your way out of. You can just "trust in the Lord with all your heart and lean not to thine own understanding."* That truth, which can sustain us in the face of unspeakable loss, can give us the strength and guidance to pursue our God-given calling during the second half of life.

Key Points of This Session

1. Each of us needs to identify and choose the one thing around which everything else in our life will flow. This mainspring is the source of our values and gives purpose to our lives. It is the overarching vision that shapes us and guides the investment of our talents, time, and treasure. Too often, people don't discover what's in the box and try to fill that void with pursuits that offer only temporary relief. That's why it is so important to clear a little space in our lives and discover the one thing that is most important to us.

2. It's impossible to journey from success to significance without addressing deeper spiritual issues. As we approach or find ourselves in halftime, we must carefully consider the role we will allow God to play in our lives. Our view of God and our response to him color our view of the possibilities ahead of us and the level of our personal involvement. Thus it is important to establish a solid foundation of beliefs from which our attitudes, values, and actions will flow. That foundation begins with a personal relationship with God through Jesus Christ.

Session Outline (55 minutes)

    I. **Introduction** (5 minutes)
    Welcome
    What's to Come
    Questions to Think About

    II. **Video Presentation: "What's in the Box?"** (19 minutes)

    III. **Group Discovery** (26 minutes)
    Video Highlights (5 minutes)
    Large Group Exploration (8 minutes)
       Pause for Personal Reflection
    Small Group Exploration (8 minutes)
       Pause for Personal Reflection
    Group Discussion (5 minutes)

    IV. **Action Points** (4 minutes)

    V. **Closing Meditation** (1 minute)

Materials

You'll need a VCR, television set, and a Bible, but no additional materials. Simply view the video segment prior to leading the session so you are familiar with its main points.

3

What's in the Box?

The thing is to understand myself, to see what God really wishes me to do ... to find the idea for which I can live and die.

Søren Kierkegaard

INTRODUCTION

5 minutes

Welcome

> Call the participants together. Welcome them to *Halftime* session 3, "What's in the Box?"

What's to Come

When Bob Buford reached a turning point during his early forties, he met with a strategic planner to sort out what he was going to do next. At one point in their discussions, the planner drew a box on a piece of paper and said, "I'm going to ask you what's in the box. For you, it is either money or Jesus Christ. If you can tell me which it is, I can tell you the strategic planning implications of that choice. If you can't tell me, you are going to oscillate between those two values and be confused for a lifetime."

That simple, penetrating question, "What's in the box?" challenged Bob to determine the one thing—the core value or belief, the primary loyalty, the overriding desire, the most essential part of himself—that would provide a sense of purpose and direction to motivate him for the second half of his life.

Today, we'll consider what belongs in our box. We'll each seek to identify the one thing that gives purpose to our lives and to establish a solid foundation of belief from which our attitudes, values, and actions will flow.

Session

3

What's in the Box?

The thing is to understand myself, to see what God really wishes me to do ... to find the idea for which I can live and die.

Søren Kierkegaard

55

PLANNING NOTES

Questions to Think About

> **Have participants open their Participant's Guide to page 56.**
>
> **As time permits, ask two or more of the following questions and solicit responses from the participants.**

Let's begin this session by considering a few questions.

 1. During our previous session, we talked about exploring possibilities that could lead to a significant second half. What are your feelings as you consider what would make your life significant?

Possible Answers: These will vary. Encourage participants to share their feelings with the group. Some individuals may be very excited, very confident about where the halftime process is leading them. Others may be confused, puzzled, or even frustrated. Some may seem to race through the process, while others will take months—even years—to go through it. Remind participants that everyone's halftime journey is unique. Encourage them to appreciate and learn from each other's journey.

 2. As we consider the possibilities for a successful second half, why might it be important for each of us to narrow our focus and identify the one thing—the core value or belief, the primary loyalty, the overriding desire—that will provide purpose, direction, and motivation for the second half of our lives?

Possible Answers: Our problem is not that we can't find anything significant to do; it is that we have so many options available to us. Until we realize what really motivates us and what we value most highly, we'll find ourselves wrestling with competing loyalties and priorities. Halftime gives us the opportunity to evaluate key issues and to identify our priorities and goals. If we don't know where we are going, chances are we'll never get there.

 3. What are some of the things that motivate people, consciously or unconsciously, to pursue specific directions?

Possible Answers: These will vary and may include desiring to obtain money, fame, pleasure, and strong family relationships; seeking a better relationship with God; a need to prove that they are successful; wanting to help people; fear of failure; desiring a secure financial future, etc.

 4. To what extent do our deepest spiritual values influence our motivation?

Possible Answers: Encourage participants to realize that, whether we admit it or not, our true spiritual values (not just our professed values) greatly influence our life pursuits. Like it or not, most of us live out the values we hold

QUESTIONS TO THINK ABOUT

1. During our previous session, we talked about exploring possibilities that could lead to a significant second half. What are your feelings as you consider what would make your life significant?

2. As we consider the possibilities for a successful second half, why might it be important for each of us to narrow our focus and identify the one thing—the core value or belief, the primary loyalty, the overriding desire—that will provide purpose, direction, and motivation for the second half of our lives?

3. What are some of the things that motivate people, consciously or unconsciously, to pursue specific directions?

4. To what extent do our deepest spiritual values influence our motivation?

HALFTIME CLIP

When we look back on the twentieth century, the thing that is going to have the greatest impact is not going to be technology, as we now assume. Rather, it will be the fact that we have an infinite array of options.

—PETER DRUCKER

PLANNING NOTES

most dear, even if we claim allegiance to different values. If we say we are concerned about the education of inner-city kids, for example, and spend our time playing golf and going to the theater but never seem to have time to help out in a tutoring program, donate time and money to programs that provide educational opportunities for economically disadvantaged kids, or advocate the improvement of inner-city schools, our professed value is questionable.

Let's keep these ideas in mind as we view the video segment. There is space in your Participant's Guide for taking notes.

HALFTIME CLIP

When we look back on the twentieth century, the thing that is going to have the greatest impact is not going to be technology, as we now assume. Rather, it will be the fact that we have an infinite array of options.

—PETER DRUCKER

VIDEO PRESENTATION: "What's in the Box?"

19
minutes

Leader's Video Observations
"What's in the Box?"

Karol's discovery

Jim's discovery

Crises that lead us to ask the question, "What's in the box?"

4. To what extent do our deepest spiritual values influence our motivation?

HALFTIME CLIP

When we look back on the twentieth century, the thing that is going to have the greatest impact is not going to be technology, as we now assume. Rather, it will be the fact that we have an infinite array of options.

—PETER DRUCKER

VIDEO NOTES

"What's in the box?"

Karol's discovery

Jim's discovery

Crises that lead us to ask the question, "What's in the box?"

PLANNING NOTES

GROUP DISCOVERY

26

minutes

> If your group has seven or more members, use the **Video Highlights** (5 minutes) with the entire group, then complete the **Large Group Exploration** (8 minutes), then break into small groups of three to five people for the **Small Group Exploration** (8 minutes). Finally, bring everyone together for the closing **Group Discussion** (5 minutes).
>
> If your group has fewer than seven members, begin with the **Video Highlights** (5 minutes), then complete both the **Large Group Exploration** (8 minutes) and the **Small Group Exploration** (8 minutes) as a group. Wrap up your discovery time with the **Group Discussion** (5 minutes).

Video Highlights (5 minutes)

> As time permits, ask one or more of the following questions that directly relate to the video segment the participants have just seen.

 1. Why is it important to discover the one thing in your box?

Possible Answers: For some participants, the thought of putting just one thing in the box will be new. So it's important that they recognize the value of discovering what is in the box and making a commitment to live accordingly. Without knowing what's in the box, we may find ourselves wavering, unable to make key decisions and stick with them, unsure of what is truly significant, and uncertain of how to fulfill our God-given calling.

 2. Karol Emmerich spoke of having inklings of profound boredom even though she lived a very successful and exciting life. In what ways have you experienced such inklings? What are your clues that life as you live it now isn't enough to satisfy you?

Possible Answers: Encourage participants to use Karol's experience as a starting point for their own self-discovery. Encourage them to share their experiences with the group so that other people will more readily recognize the signs of halftime in their lives.

 3. Jim Thweatt gets excited about helping kids who are headed for failure to stay in school, learn, and prosper. When he talks about these kids, it's easy to see where his treasure is. It is easy to see what is in his box. Why is what's in his box an important idea for Jim?

Possible Answers: One way to describe what's in Jim's box is to say that it is building treasure in heaven rather than on earth. This is what motivates Jim to give his time and energy to inner-city kids. When he wonders if he is off track because, for example, all of his friends make more money than he

SESSION THREE: What's in the Box? **59**

VIDEO HIGHLIGHTS

1. Why is it important to discover the one thing in your box?

2. Karol Emmerich spoke of having inklings of profound boredom even though she lived a very successful and exciting life. In what ways have you experienced such inklings? What are your clues that life as you live it now isn't enough to satisfy you?

3. Jim Thweatt gets excited about helping kids who are headed for failure to stay in school, learn, and prosper. When he talks about these kids, it's easy to see where his treasure is. It is easy to see what is in his box. Why is what's in his box an important idea for Jim?

PLANNING NOTES

does, building treasure in heaven is the central idea that redirects him toward his purpose, that reminds him of what is significant.

 4. Like Tim Sambrano and Rogers Kirven, most of us think we will be satisfied and happy once we have successfully achieved our dreams. Yet they discovered the dark side of halftime—the frustration and uncertainty of living without direction, of living a life that lacks significance. What are the implications of their discovery for your life?

Possible Answers: Many people are unaware that achieving one's dreams has a downside. Encourage participants to express their perceptions of what the dark side of halftime could be and to explore how it might affect them.

HALFTIME CLIP

Significance begins by stopping wherever you are in the journey to see what's in the box, and then reordering your life around its contents.   **—BOB BUFORD**

Large Group Exploration (8 minutes)

Discovering What's in Our Box

We've seen a glimpse of how important it is for each of us to choose the one thing in our box—the one thing that will provide motivation and purpose for the second half of our lives. Some people choose family, money, or career. Bob Buford chose Jesus Christ. Regardless of what is, or has been, in our box, let's talk about the process of discovering what we really want to put into our box.

Perhaps we have made that choice already. Perhaps we have allowed other people or circumstances to make that choice for us. But it's never too late for each of us to evaluate what's in our box and see if what has been the one thing should stay there or be replaced.

 1. What are some common beliefs and core values around which people build their lives?

Possible Answers: Encourage participants to see not only the great variety of core beliefs and values around which people build their lives but also some of the consequences of choosing those values and beliefs. Some people choose fame, money, pleasure, power, and/or status. Some people pursue God and seek to obey him and live out their faith daily. Other people build their lives around their families, New Age philosophies, thrill seeking,

60   HALFTIME PARTICIPANT'S GUIDE

4. Like Tim Sambrano and Rogers Kirven, most of us think we will be satisfied and happy once we have successfully achieved our dreams. Yet they discovered the dark side of halftime—the frustration and uncertainty of living without direction, of living a life that lacks significance. What are the implications of their discovery for your life?

HALFTIME CLIP

Significance begins by stopping wherever you are in the journey to see what's in the box, and then reordering your life around its contents.
—**BOB BUFORD**

SESSION THREE: What's in the Box?   **61**

LARGE GROUP EXPLORATION

Discovering What's in Our Box

We've seen a glimpse of how important it is for each of us to choose the one thing in our box—the one thing that will provide motivation and purpose for the second half of our lives. Some people choose family, money, or career. Bob Buford chose Jesus Christ. Regardless of what is, or has been, in our box, let's talk about the process of discovering what we really want to put into our box.

Perhaps we have made that choice already. Perhaps we have allowed other people or circumstances to make that choice for us. But it's never too late for each of us to evaluate what's in our box and see if what has been the one thing should stay there or be replaced.

1. What are some of the common beliefs and core values around which people build their lives?

2. Let's say person A decides that the one thing in his or her box is money—achieving financial freedom by a specific age. Person B, on the other hand, has put making a difference in the lives of disadvantaged young people in the box. Although individual situations obviously vary, let's consider some of the ways in which person A and person B might make different decisions in the following areas.

---

political or social causes, or careers. Still other people, although they may not call it a value, structure their lives around escapism, which could include excessive drinking, sexual addiction, gambling, and other addictions.

 2. Let's say person A decides that the one thing in his or her box is money—achieving financial freedom by a specific age. Person B, on the other hand, has put making a difference in the lives of disadvantaged young people in the box. Although individual situations obviously vary, let's consider some of the ways in which person A and person B might make different decisions in the following areas.

Decision Area	Person A: Financial Freedom	Person B: Helping Young People
Family Life Involvement	*may be driven to achieve at work and spend little time with his or her family; may consider the goal of making money to be the most important thing to give his or her family*	*may spend a great deal of time with young people—playing sports with them, hanging out, etc.—that may infringe on personal or family time; may include these young people in family life activities*
Dedication to Career	*may spend most of his or her time working—or thinking about work-related issues; may become a workaholic who neglects other areas of life; may be tempted to cut corners ethically to meet his or her goals*	*may make a career of helping these young people; may seek a less-demanding career that allows time to invest in kids; may even neglect his or her job responsibilities to do what he or she considers more important*
Use of Personal Time	*is likely to spend lots of time thinking about or making money—juggling deals to maximize financial returns; will often evaluate outside activities in terms of their potential to serve his or her overriding financial goals*	*is likely to use personal time to build relationships with young people; may think continually of ways to connect with kids on a deeper level; may spend time praying for the kids; may recruit other friends to help*
Use of Financial Resources	*considers return on investment above all other factors; may find it difficult to put money into projects that don't have a clear bottom line*	*views money as a resource that can be invested in the lives of kids; considers any return to be worth the investment*
Use of Talents	*may focus his or her talents on accumulating financial resources, gaining financial-related expertise*	*may focus his or her talents on meeting specific needs, teaching specific skills, offering a listening ear and advice to troubled kids, promoting the cause in order to raise funds*

LARGE GROUP EXPLORATION

Discovering What's in Our Box

We've seen a glimpse of how important it is for each of us to choose the one thing in our box—the one thing that will provide motivation and purpose for the second half of our lives. Some people choose family, money, or career. Bob Buford chose Jesus Christ. Regardless of what is, or has been, in our box, let's talk about the process of discovering what we really want to put into our box.

Perhaps we have made that choice already. Perhaps we have allowed other people or circumstances to make that choice for us. But it's never too late for each of us to evaluate what's in our box and see if what has been the one thing should stay there or be replaced.

1. What are some of the common beliefs and core values around which people build their lives?

2. Let's say person A decides that the one thing in his or her box is money—achieving financial freedom by a specific age. Person B, on the other hand, has put making a difference in the lives of disadvantaged young people in the box. Although individual situations obviously vary, let's consider some of the ways in which person A and person B might make different decisions in the following areas.

Decision Area	Person A: Financial Freedom	Person B: Helping Young People
Family Life Involvement		
Dedication to Career		
Use of Personal Time		
Use of Financial Resources		
Use of Talents		

3. What are some of the obstacles that may make it difficult for a person to put that one thing of his or her choosing into the box?

PLANNING NOTES

3. What are some of the obstacles that may make it difficult for a person to put that one thing of his or her choosing into the box?

Possible Answers: fear of upsetting the status quo, failing to meet the expectations of family members and/or friends, not knowing what that one thing is, having a difficult time reconciling conflicting values or beliefs, not wanting to choose between two or more appealing options, not wanting to face the requirements and implications of that choice, being too busy to stop and think about personal issues, etc.

 4. Do you think everyone who seriously evaluates what's in his or her box must also address such spiritual questions as, "Where is God in my life?" "What is God doing, and what plans might he have for me?" "Is it enough to live for myself?" Why or why not?

Possible Answers: These will vary. Some individuals will find it essential to answer the spiritual questions as they move through the halftime process. For other people, spiritual questions take a back seat. But in the final analysis, everyone who experiences a successful halftime needs to decide how important spiritual issues will be in his or her life—and make choices accordingly. Someone who doesn't believe that God has a plan for his or her life will naturally go through a different process than someone who turns to God for guidance and help.

 5. Bob Buford has said, "You can keep the box empty for only so long. If you do not choose the one thing that belongs in the box, life's inertia will choose it for you." What does he mean by this statement? How does it impact your halftime choices?

Possible Answers: Encourage participants to discuss the implications of not addressing the question, "What's in the box?" Our surroundings—culture, family, peers—exert subtle as well as blatant pressures on us to live a certain way. So if we don't know the one thing that belongs in our box, we will, as the consultant told Bob Buford, oscillate between values. Furthermore, the pulls in life tend to guide us toward predetermined destinations. We need to *choose* to take the path that leads to the fulfillment of God's calling for our lives.

HALFTIME CLIP

Your "one thing" is the most essential part of you, your transcendent dimension. It is discovering what's true about yourself, rather than overlaying someone else's truth on you or injecting someone else's goals onto your personality.
—BOB BUFORD

Decision Area	Person A: Financial Freedom	Person B: Helping Young People
Family Life Involvement		
Dedication to Career		
Use of Personal Time		
Use of Financial Resources		
Use of Talents		

3. What are some of the obstacles that may make it difficult for a person to put that one thing of his or her choosing into the box?

4. Do you think everyone who seriously evaluates what's in his or her box must also address such spiritual questions as, "Where is God in my life?" "What is God doing, and what plans might he have for me?" "Is it enough to live for myself?" Why or why not?

5. Bob Buford has said, "You can keep the box empty for only so long. If you do not choose the one thing that belongs in the box, life's inertia will choose it for you." What does he mean by this statement? How does it impact your halftime choices?

HALFTIME CLIP

Your "one thing" is the most essential part of you, your transcendent dimension. It is discovering what's true about yourself, rather than overlaying someone else's truth on you or injecting someone else's goals onto your personality.
—BOB BUFORD

PLANNING NOTES

What's in My Box?

Some of us, like Karol Emmerich, seem almost instinctively to know what belongs in the box. For others of us, it is a challenge to discover the one thing that belongs in the box. If you find yourself struggling to identify what belongs in your box, spend some time answering the following questions when this session is over. Be as specific as you can. You might know more about what's important to you than you realize!

What makes me tick?	
What is my passion, the spark that needs only a little breeze to ignite into a raging fire?	
What do I enjoy so much that I'd do it without pay?	
Which thing(s) outside my box have screamed for my attention?	
Where am I in my life now?	
Where do I want to be? What do I want to be doing in ten years? In twenty years?	
What gives me a deep sense of satisfaction and purpose?	
What do I feel I am missing in my life?	
Which God-given gifts have I perfected through the years?	
Which God-given gifts have I been unable to use much—or at all?	
What is difficult about choosing what's in my box—and living that way?	
Which regrets or mistakes may be holding me back from discovering what's in my box?	
What cause much bigger than my own personal concerns is worth living or dying for?	
What's in my box now? Do I want that to remain there?	
In what way(s) does my view of God influence what's in my box right now?	

HALFTIME DRILL

What's in My Box?
Some of us, like Karol Emmerich, seem almost instinctively to know what belongs box. For others of us, it is a challenge to discover the one thing that belongs in the box. If you find yourself struggling to identify what belongs in your box, spend some time answering the following questions when this session is over. Be as specific as you can. You might know more about what's important to you than you realize!

What makes me tick?	
What is my passion, the spark that needs only a little breeze to ignite into a raging fire?	
What do I enjoy so much that I'd do it without pay?	
Which thing(s) outside my box have screamed for my attention?	
Where am I in my life now?	
Where do I want to be? What do I want to be doing in ten years? In twenty years?	
What gives me a deep sense of satisfaction and purpose?	
What do I feel I am missing in my life?	

Which God-given gifts have I perfected through the years?	
Which God-given gifts have I been unable to use much—or at all?	
What is difficult about choosing what's in my box—and living that way?	
Which regrets or mistakes may be holding me back from discovering what's in my box?	
What cause much bigger than my own personal concerns is worth living or dying for?	
What's in my box now? Do I want that to remain there?	
In what way(s) does my view of God influence what's in my box right now?	

PLANNING NOTES

Pause for Personal Reflection

Now it's time to pause to consider what might be in our respective boxes and to think about what God might be trying to say to each of us.

- If someone asked me to reveal the one thing that motivates me, what would I say?
- If my family members and/or friends were asked what motivates me, what would they say? How would their answers differ from mine?
- How important a role do my core values and beliefs play in my daily decisions? (Be honest!)
- How much time am I willing to devote to answering the question, "What's in my box?"

Let participants know when there is one minute remaining.

HALFTIME CLIP

No amount of activity will ever satisfy the longing to find the one thing that is uniquely yours—the thing that, once found, will enable you to make a difference. **—BOB BUFORD**

66   HALFTIME PARTICIPANT'S GUIDE

Pause for Personal Reflection

Now it's time to pause to consider what might be in our respective boxes and to think about what God might be trying to say to each of us.

If someone asked me to reveal the one thing that motivates me, what would I say?

If my family members and/or friends were asked what motivates me, what would they say? How would their answers differ from mine?

How important a role do my core values and beliefs play in my daily decisions? (Be honest!)

SESSION THREE: What's in the Box?   **67**

How much time am I willing to devote to answering the question, "What's in my box?"

HALFTIME CLIP

No amount of activity will ever satisfy the longing to find the one thing that is uniquely yours—the thing that, once found, will enable you to make a difference.

—BOB BUFORD

PLANNING NOTES

Small Group Exploration (8 minutes)

Trusting God and His Leading

Bob Buford believes it's vital for people making the journey from success to significance to address the deeper spiritual issues. As we approach or find ourselves in halftime, we must carefully consider the role we will allow God to play in our lives. Will we trust him enough, for example, to ask him to guide us toward our calling and rejoice in the opportunity to pursue a significant second half?

Look up the following verses and discuss their implications for you as you move through the halftime process.

 1. Psalm 46:1–3; Isaiah 40:28–31; 58:11

Possible Answers: God desires to satisfy, strengthen, and protect us. Thus we are not alone as we take risks and seek to discover his calling for us. We can count on more than ourselves or other people; we can turn to him when things become difficult.

 2. Psalm 29:11; Isaiah 26:3; Philippians 4:6–7

Possible Answers: God offers us his peace. It is a gift he gives, no matter how difficult things may be. We can be peaceful when we trust in him. Instead of being anxious and worried, we can present our needs to him, and his peace will guard our hearts and minds.

 3. Proverbs 3:5–6; James 1:5–6

Possible Answers: If we ask him without doubting, God will give us wisdom and guidance. We don't have to figure out everything on our own. And if we trust him fully rather than making our decisions without him, God will lead us along the right paths. (Note: Some of the ways God provides wisdom and guidance include the Bible, the wise counsel of godly people, and the Holy Spirit within us.)

 4. Lamentations 3:25; Matthew 7:7–11; James 5:16b–18; 1 John 5:14–15

Possible Answers: God listens to and responds to our prayers when we seek him and his will for our lives. We can bring all of our needs before him, and he will respond. So we can bring our halftime decisions before him. Sometimes he will open doors. Sometimes he will say no. Sometimes he will want us to wait. No matter what his answer, he has our best interests at heart.

 5. Psalm 36:5; 1 Corinthians 1:9; Hebrews 10:23

68   HALFTIME PARTICIPANT'S GUIDE

SMALL GROUP EXPLORATION

Trusting God and His Leading
Bob Buford believes it's vital for people making the journey from success to significance to address the deeper spiritual issues. As we approach or find ourselves in halftime, we must carefully consider the role we will allow God to play in our lives. Will we trust him enough, for example, to ask him to guide us toward our calling and rejoice in the opportunity to pursue a significant second half?

Look up the following verses and discuss their implications for you as you move through the halftime process.

1. Psalm 46:1–3; Isaiah 40:28–31; 58:11

2. Psalm 29:11; Isaiah 26:3; Philippians 4:6–7

3. Proverbs 3:5–6; James 1:5–6

SESSION THREE: What's in the Box?   **69**

4. Lamentations 3:25; Matthew 7:7–11; James 5:16b–18; 1 John 5:14–15

5. Psalm 36:5; 1 Corinthians 1:9; Hebrews 10:23

6. Psalm 130:3–4; Colossians 2:13–15; 1 John 1:9

HALFTIME CLIP

Remember, you can have only one thing in the box. Regardless of your position in life, once you have identified what's in your box, you will be able to see the cluster of activities—surrounded by quiet times for spiritual disciplines, reading, and reflecting—that put into play your one thing and keep you growing.
—BOB BUFORD

PLANNING NOTES

Possible Answers: God is loving and faithful. We can count on him to keep his promises. He will stand with us, which provides great hope as we confront the challenges of halftime.

 6. Psalm 130:3–4; Colossians 2:13–15; 1 John 1:9

Possible Answers: God will forgive us when we confess our sins to him. No matter what we have done, we can be cleansed of our sins through what Jesus accomplished on the cross and can have a dynamic relationship with God. Halftime can be a time to receive forgiveness and start out fresh in new directions. We don't have to carry the baggage of our past.

HALFTIME CLIP

> *Remember, you can have only one thing in the box. Regardless of your position in life, once you have identified what's in your box, you will be able to see the cluster of activities—surrounded by quiet times for spiritual disciplines, reading, and reflecting—that put into play your one thing and keep you growing.*
>
> —BOB BUFORD

Pause for Personal Reflection

Now it's time to pause to consider what role we will allow God to play as we go through halftime.

- People in the video segment mentioned the importance of God in their lives. Am I actively seeking his calling for my life, or am I pursuing other things? As I evaluate what's in my box, where does God fit in?
- What does my life look like from God's perspective? If God audibly spoke to me about my mission in life, what do I think he would say?
- How is my view of God influencing my response to halftime?
- Do I believe what the Bible says about God enough to risk discovering what he has for me during the second half of my life? Why or why not?

> Let participants know when there is one minute remaining.

HALFTIME DRILL

4. Lamentations 3:25; Matthew 7:7–11; James 5:16b–18; 1 John 5:14–15

5. Psalm 36:5; 1 Corinthians 1:9; Hebrews 10:23

6. Psalm 130:3–4; Colossians 2:13–15; 1 John 1:9

HALFTIME CLIP

Remember, you can have only one thing in the box. Regardless of your position in life, once you have identified what's in your box, you will be able to see the cluster of activities—surrounded by quiet times for spiritual disciplines, reading, and reflecting—that put into play your one thing and keep you growing.

—BOB BUFORD

Pause for Personal Reflection

Now it's time to pause to consider what role we will allow God to play as we go through halftime.

People in the video segment mentioned the importance of God in their lives. Am I actively seeking his calling for my life, or am I pursuing other things? As I evaluate what's in my box, where does God fit in?

What does my life look like from God's perspective? If God audibly spoke to me about my mission in life, what do I think he would say?

How is my view of God influencing my response to halftime?

Do I believe what the Bible says about God enough to risk discovering what he has for me during the second half of my life? Why or why not?

PLANNING NOTES

In Which Spiritual-Belief Category Do You Fit?

As you seek to identify what belongs in your box and to explore the role your spiritual beliefs will play during your second half, it will be helpful to examine your level of spiritual belief and commitment and consider how it influences your halftime experience.

Which Spiritual-Belief Category Am I In?	How Is It Influencing My Goal to Discover What's in My Box?
Noncommitted. I believe in God, but seldom talk about it and rarely attend church. I am unfamiliar with the Bible.	
Creedal believer. I made a public acknowledgment of belief at one time and consider myself to be aligned with a religious movement or denomination. I attend church infrequently, usually on holidays.	
Active believer. I attend church regularly. I volunteer. I know quite a bit of religious teaching and have some biblical knowledge, but I am uncomfortable articulating my spiritual beliefs. I practice my religion within the church walls.	
Committed believer. I would describe my spiritual beliefs in terms of a personal relationship with God through Jesus Christ. I have a deeply spiritual life, regularly praying and reading the Bible. I'm comfortable talking about personal beliefs and helping other people learn more about their faith. I lead a life of service. I am active in church but don't equate church activities with a personal relationship with God.	

HALFTIME CLIP

Don't let the fact that you have to work for a living limit the grace God has in store for you during your second half. Don't allow the second half of your life to be characterized by decline, boredom, and increasing ineffectiveness for the kingdom. Listen carefully to that gentle whisper and then do some honest soul-searching. What's in your box? Is it money? Career? Family? Freedom?
—BOB BUFORD

HALFTIME DRILL

In Which Spiritual-Belief Category Do You Fit?

As you seek to identify what belongs in your box and to explore the role your spiritual beliefs will play during your second half, it will be helpful to examine your level of spiritual belief and commitment and consider how it influences your halftime experience.

Which Spiritual-Belief Category Am I In?	How Is It Influencing My Goal to Discover What's in My Box?
Noncommitted. I believe in God, but seldom talk about it and rarely attend church. I am unfamiliar with the Bible.	
Creedal believer. I made a public acknowledgment of belief at one time and consider myself to be aligned with a religious movement or denomination. I attend church infrequently, usually on holidays.	
Active believer. I attend church regularly. I volunteer. I know quite a bit of religious teaching and have some biblical knowledge, but I am uncomfortable articulating my spiritual beliefs. I practice my religion within the church walls.	
Committed believer. I would describe my spiritual beliefs in terms of a personal relationship with God through Jesus Christ. I have a deeply spiritual life, regularly praying and reading the Bible. I'm comfortable talking about personal beliefs and helping other people learn more about their faith. I lead a life of service. I am active in church but don't equate church activities with a personal relationship with God.	

HALFTIME CLIP

Don't let the fact that you have to work for a living limit the grace God has in store for you during your second half. Don't allow the second half of your life to be characterized by decline, boredom, and increasing ineffectiveness for the kingdom. Listen carefully to that gentle whisper and then do some honest soul-searching. What's in your box? Is it money? Career? Family? Freedom?   **—BOB BUFORD**

Group Discussion (5 minutes)

Now it's time to wrap up our discovery time.

> Give participants a moment to transition from their thoughtfulness and begin sharing their observations with the entire group. Use the following questions as discussion starters.

Bob Buford writes, "The first half of life has to do with getting and gaining, learning and earning.... The second half is more risky because it has to do with living beyond the immediate. It is about releasing the seed of creativity and energy that has been implanted within us, watering and cultivating it so that we may be abundantly fruitful. It involves investing our gifts in service to others—and receiving the personal joy that comes as a result of that spending."

Deciding to put only one thing in the box is risky. Let's talk about some of those risks.

 1. What are the risks of "releasing the seed of creativity and energy" that has been implanted within each of us? What might the benefits be?

 2. Why do you think so much within our culture encourages us to use what we have been given—abilities, talents, financial means—to promote our own accomplishments and purposes rather than to serve other people?

 3. What is the difference between being driven to achieve and being called purposefully toward one's destiny?

 4. Do you agree or disagree with the statement, "The forces of evil would like nothing more than to prevent talented, productive people committed to God from becoming their truest selves in service to their Creator"? Why or why not?

GROUP DISCUSSION

Bob Buford writes, "The first half of life has to do with getting and gaining, learning and earning.... The second half is more risky because it has to do with living beyond the immediate. It is about releasing the seed of creativity and energy that has been implanted within us, watering and cultivating it so that we may be abundantly fruitful. It involves investing our gifts in service to others—and receiving the personal joy that comes as a result of that spending."

Deciding to put only one thing in the box is risky. Let's talk about some of those risks.

1. What are the risks of "releasing the seed of creativity and energy" that has been implanted within each of us? What might the benefits be?

2. Why do you think so much within our culture encourages us to use what we have been given—abilities, talents, financial means—to promote our own accomplishments and purposes rather than to serve other people?

3. What is the difference between being driven to achieve and being called purposefully toward one's destiny?

4. Do you agree or disagree with the statement, "The forces of evil would like nothing more than to prevent talented, productive people committed to God from becoming their truest selves in service to their Creator"? Why or why not?

PLANNING NOTES

ACTION POINTS

minutes

The following points are reproduced on page xx of the Participant's Guide.

I'd like to take a moment to summarize the key points we explored today. After I have reviewed these points, I will give you a moment to consider what you will commit to do as a result of what you have discovered during this session.

Read the following points and pause afterward so participants can consider and write out their commitments.

 1. Each of us needs to identify and choose the one thing around which everything else in our life will flow. This mainspring is the source of our values and gives purpose to our lives. It is the overarching vision that shapes us and guides the investment of our talents, time, and treasure. Too often, people don't discover what's in the box and try to fill that void with pursuits that offer only temporary relief. That's why it is so important to clear a little space in our lives and discover the one thing that is most important to us.

Take time now to think about what's in your box. Is it fame? Money? God? Family? Career?

Perhaps you cannot yet write the one or two words that summarize what's in your box. If you are undecided, at least write down what you consider your options to be.

 2. It's impossible to journey from success to significance without addressing deeper spiritual issues. As we approach or find ourselves in halftime, we must carefully consider the role we will allow God to play in our lives. Our view of God and our response to him color our view of the possibilities ahead of us and the level of our personal involvement. Thus it is important to establish a solid foundation of beliefs from which our attitudes, values, and actions will flow. That foundation begins with a personal relationship with God through Jesus Christ.

Set aside some quiet time to consider the following questions:

1. **In what way(s) am I satisfied and dissatisfied with my spiritual beliefs?**

ACTION POINTS

What will you commit to do as a result of what you have discovered during this session?

1. Each of us needs to identify and choose the one thing around which everything else in our life will flow. This mainspring is the source of our values and gives purpose to our lives. It is the overarching vision that shapes us and guides the investment of our talents, time, and treasure. Too often, people don't discover what's in the box and try to fill that void with pursuits that offer only temporary relief. That's why it is so important to clear a little space in our lives and discover the one thing that is most important to us.

   Take time now to think about what's in your box. Is it fame? Money? God? Family? Career?

   Perhaps you cannot yet write the one or two words that summarize what's in your box. If you are undecided, at least write down what you consider your options to be.

2. It's impossible to journey from success to significance without addressing deeper spiritual issues. As we approach or find ourselves in halftime, we must carefully consider the role we will allow God to play in our lives. Our view of God and our response to him color our view of the possibilities ahead of us and the level of our personal involvement. Thus it is important to establish a solid foundation of beliefs from which our attitudes, values, and actions will flow. That foundation begins with a personal relationship with God through Jesus Christ.

   Set aside some quiet time to consider the following questions:

   1. **In what way(s) am I satisfied and dissatisfied with my spiritual beliefs?**

   2. **To what extent do my spiritual beliefs determine what I do and how I think? To what extent do they provide a solid foundation on which I can build a significant second half?**

PLANNING NOTES

2. To what extent do my spiritual beliefs determine what I do and how I think? To what extent do they provide a solid foundation on which I can build a significant second half?

3. For what do I need to trust God as I make a commitment to place my one thing in the box?

HALFTIME CLIP

I have hesitated, at times, to tell my story. I have been so uniquely blessed that I don't want anyone to conclude that only rich guys can have a better second half. Please remember that my second half is going well not because I have money but because I swallowed hard and put one thing in the box. It was not easy for me to do, nor will it be easy for you, either. But that is what has made the difference.
—BOB BUFORD

CLOSING MEDITATION

minute

Dear God, thank you for loving each of us just the way we are and for the plans you have already made for each of us. Please guide each of us as we think about what's in our box and make key choices for our future. You know it's not easy for us to face the issues deep inside us. Help us to remember that you are with us during this halftime process—providing hope, wisdom, and guidance. If anyone in this group today does not yet know you as Lord and Savior, may he or she be drawn closer to you today. In your name we pray, Jesus, amen.

76　　HALFTIME PARTICIPANT'S GUIDE

2. It's impossible to journey from success to significance without addressing deeper spiritual issues. As we approach or find ourselves in halftime, we must carefully consider the role we will allow God to play in our lives. Our view of God and our response to him color our view of the possibilities ahead of us and the level of our personal involvement. Thus it is important to establish a solid foundation of beliefs from which our attitudes, values, and actions will flow. That foundation begins with a personal relationship with God through Jesus Christ.

Set aside some quiet time to consider the following questions:

1. In what way(s) am I satisfied and dissatisfied with my spiritual beliefs?

2. To what extent do my spiritual beliefs determine what I do and how I think? To what extent do they provide a solid foundation on which I can build a significant second half?

3. For what do I need to trust God as I make a commitment to place my one thing in the box?

HALFTIME CLIP

I have hesitated, at times, to tell my story. I have been so uniquely blessed that I don't want anyone to conclude that only rich guys can have a better second half. Please remember that my second half is going well not because I have money but because I swallowed hard and put one thing in the box. It was not easy for me to do, nor will it be easy for you, either. But that is what has made the difference.

—BOB BUFORD

PLANNING NOTES

What God Views as Significant

People try to find significance in various ways. We need only to look around us—and in our own lives—to see the consequences of those pursuits. Let's take a look at what God views as significant.

Look up the following verses and write out what they reveal about God's perspective on what's important.

Scripture	What God Views as Significant
Matthew 25:31–40; James 1:27	
Isaiah 57:15; Micah 6:8; Matthew 18:1–4; 23:12	
Leviticus 20:26; Psalm 97:10; Romans 13:12–14; 2 Timothy 2:19, 22	
Mark 12:28–31	
2 Timothy 4:7–8; Hebrews 11:6	
Matthew 5:38–47; Luke 6:32–35; Hebrews 13:16	
Psalm 11:7; 33:5; Jeremiah 9:24	

HALFTIME DRILL

What God Views as Significant

People try to find significance in various ways. We need only to look around us—and in our own lives—to see the consequences of those pursuits. Let's take a look at what God views as significant.

Look up the following verses and write out what they reveal about God's perspective on what's important.

Scripture	What God Views as Significant
Matthew 25:31–40; James 1:27	
Isaiah 57:15; Micah 6:8; Matthew 18:1–4; 23:12	
Leviticus 20:26; Psalm 97:10; Romans 13:12–14; 2 Timothy 2:19, 22	
Mark 12:28–31	
2 Timothy 4:7–8; Hebrews 11:6	
Matthew 5:38–47; Luke 6:32–35; Hebrews 13:16	
Psalm 11:7; 33:5; Jeremiah 9:24	

PLANNING NOTES

4

Game Plan for Significance

BEFORE YOU LEAD

Synopsis

During this session, you'll guide participants in taking key steps that will help them chart a course toward significance. These practical steps involve developing a personal mission statement and clearing the plate so they can each begin to discover and live out their life's mission.

The video segment for this session focuses on the life of Clare DeGraaf, who at age thirty-two was living the American dream. The owner of a successful company, he was at the top of his game. There was nowhere to go but up. Then Clare was diagnosed with lymphoma. As he considered the ramifications of his illness, he wondered what people would write on his gravestone, what difference his life had made. So while their friends were establishing families and building careers, Clare and Sue DeGraaf faced halftime.

Clare knew about Christianity, but he wasn't a Christian. What's more, he was afraid to become one. "I was a leadership kind of person," he says. "I didn't want to have to sell my Mercedes or go off to the mission field in Nigeria." Yet he invited Jesus Christ to become his Lord and Savior and hoped that God wouldn't "do anything crazy" with him.

Following a two-and-a-half-hour prayer service, Clare's cancer was gone. He had a new life to live and a key decision to make. Would he take a new path and walk away from the job that had consumed virtually his every waking moment, or would he remain on the same familiar path?

During the next three years, he began sharing the biblical concepts he was learning with other people, and, as he puts it, "God changed the desires of my heart." The man whose business had captured his heart no longer had a heart for his business. He had a new mission. Sensing that God was calling him into ministry, Clare sold his business. He walked away, not knowing if he could even do what God was calling him to do.

Today, Clare has a passionate relationship with God, has meaning and purpose in life, and is living a life of significance. He has found the mission God designed specifically for him—investing his energy and passion into people's lives. He conducts Bible studies and meets one-on-one with top business professionals. He has helped to build orphanages and hospitals in Albania, serves in his local church, and assists ministries such as Door, a ministry to the deaf community.

Clare DeGraaf has no regrets because he is fulfilling his mission, "doing something that has eternal significance." This session will help each participant develop a mission statement for his or her second half. It will also help participants take practical steps toward implementing their mission statements so that they, like Clare, can live with no regrets.

Key Points of This Session

1. Defining what's in our box is an important step in the journey from success to significance. But unless our mission matches our intention, we will experience a dissonance that ultimately will be destructive. So it is essential that we each choose a mission and formulate a personal mission statement that matches whatever we put into our box. Once we have formulated our mission statement, we can begin to establish a game plan that will lead us in the direction we want to go.

2. We don't have to live life with regrets. Instead of just staying where we are and being afraid of change, each of us—no matter what our background may be—can take risks and step toward significance. We can clear our plate of distractions and unnecessary demands and start living out our personal life missions. We can embark on the journey of doing the good works God has ordained for us to do.

Session Outline (54 minutes)

   I. **Introduction** (5 minutes)
   Welcome
   What's to Come
   Questions to Think About

   II. **Video Presentation: "Game Plan for Significance"**
   (16 minutes)

    III. **Group Discovery** (27 minutes)
        Video Highlights (5 minutes)
        Large Group Exploration (8 minutes)
          Pause for Personal Reflection
        Small Group Exploration (8 minutes)
          Pause for Personal Reflection
        Group Discussion (6 minutes)

    IV. **Action Points** (5 minutes)

    V. **Closing Meditation** (1 minute)

Materials

You'll need a VCR, television set, and a Bible, but no additional materials. Simply view the video segment prior to leading the session so you are familiar with its main points.

Session

4

Game Plan for Significance

*It is not enough to **feel** like doing something significant. The newly discovered resolve that comes when you place just one thing in the box will fade if you do not apply it to a related goal.*

Bob Buford

INTRODUCTION

minutes

Welcome

> Call the participants together. Welcome them to *Halftime* session 4, "Game Plan for Significance."

What's to Come

During this session, we'll be introduced to Sue and Clare DeGraaf, who began facing halftime when Clare was diagnosed with cancer at age thirty-two. We'll see some of the issues Clare had to wrestle with as he progressed from success to significance. We'll see how he went about developing and implementing his personal life mission. We'll see the difference his decisions have made today—in his life, the life of his family, and in the lives of other people. And we'll each start to develop our personal mission statement and begin clearing away distractions so we can fulfill our mission.

Questions to Think About

> Have participants open their Participant's Guide to page 80.
>
> As time permits, ask two or more of the following questions and solicit responses from the participants.

Let's begin this session by considering a few questions.

 1. What excites you most about the opportunities you are considering as a result of the halftime process?

Session

4

Game Plan for Significance

*It is not enough to **feel** like doing something signif-icant. The newly discovered resolve that comes when you place just one thing in the box will fade if you do not apply it to a related goal.*

Bob Buford

79

QUESTIONS TO THINK ABOUT

1. What excites you most about the opportunities you are con-sidering as a result of the halftime process?

2. What aspects of the halftime process seem a little intimidat-ing or difficult at this point?

3. What do you want to do with the one thing you put into your box? What do you see as the next step to take?

HALFTIME CLIP

Most first-halfers become victims of centrifugal force. Around the per-imeter of their lives are vital points that demand attention. ... They begin with every intention of tending to each, but in order to do that, they have to shift into a higher gear. Before long, they are spinning rap-idly around the perimeter, the resulting force driv-ing them farther and farther from the center, the core of who they are. **—BOB BUFORD**

Possible Answers: Encourage participants to share what they are thinking about. Some may be gaining confidence that they can make positive changes in their life, others may be getting in touch with God through Bible reading and prayer, some may feel excited about having discovered what's in their box, others may have found specific opportunities to pursue, etc.

 2. What aspects of the halftime process seem a little intimidating or difficult at this point?

Possible Answers: Encourage participants to honestly share their challenges. Some may be considering major changes, some may be feeling pressure from family or peers, some may wonder if God really has a calling for them, some may be concerned about the financial impact of pursuing their dreams, others may resist asking themselves the tough questions, etc.

 3. What do you want to do with the one thing you put into your box? What do you see as the next step to take?

Possible Answers: Encourage participants to dream a little, to imagine themselves actually doing something with what they have discovered, to speculate as to what their next steps toward significance might be. Some participants may be ready to launch into a new mission, others may see a number of options they need to evaluate, still others will need to make some lifestyle changes to proceed on their journey.

Let's keep these ideas in mind as we view the video segment. There is space in your Participant's Guide for taking notes.

HALFTIME CLIP

Most first-halfers become victims of centrifugal force. Around the perimeter of their lives are vital points that demand attention.... They begin with every intention of tending to each, but in order to do that, they have to shift into a higher gear. Before long, they are spinning rapidly around the perimeter, the resulting force driving them farther and farther from the center, the core of who they are.

—BOB BUFORD

QUESTIONS TO THINK ABOUT

1. What excites you most about the opportunities you are considering as a result of the halftime process?

2. What aspects of the halftime process seem a little intimidating or difficult at this point?

3. What do you want to do with the one thing you put into your box? What do you see as the next step to take?

HALFTIME CLIP

Most first-halfers become victims of centrifugal force. Around the perimeter of their lives are vital points that demand attention. ... They begin with every intention of tending to each, but in order to do that, they have to shift into a higher gear. Before long, they are spinning rapidly around the perimeter, the resulting force driving them farther and farther from the center, the core of who they are.   —BOB BUFORD

PLANNING NOTES

VIDEO PRESENTATION: "Game Plan for Significance"

16
minutes

Leader's Video Observations
Clare and Sue DeGraaf's wake-up call

A change of heart

Making a difference

Living life with no regrets

VIDEO NOTES

Clare and Sue DeGraaf's wake-up call

A change of heart

Making a difference

Living life with no regrets

PLANNING NOTES

GROUP DISCOVERY

minutes

> If your group has seven or more members, use the **Video Highlights** (5 minutes) with the entire group, then complete the **Large Group Exploration** (8 minutes), then break into small groups of three to five people for the **Small Group Exploration** (8 minutes). Finally, bring everyone together for the closing **Group Discussion** (5 minutes).
>
> If your group has fewer than seven members, begin with the **Video Highlights** (5 minutes), then complete both the **Large Group Exploration** (8 minutes) and the **Small Group Exploration** (8 minutes) as a group. Wrap up your discovery time with the **Group Discussion** (5 minutes).

Video Highlights (5 minutes)

> As time permits, ask one or more of the following questions that directly relate to the video segment the participants have just seen.

 1. What role did Clare's view of God play in his journey from success to significance?

   Possible Answers: Clare reevaluated his relationship with God when he started questioning the significance of his life. Committing himself to a personal relationship with God was for Clare a key step toward significance. This was definitely a step into the unknown, and it was a scary step for Clare to take. As his faith deepened, he was able to take greater steps away from success and toward significance.

 2. Once Clare got a taste of what it meant to allow God to guide his life, how did he respond? How might what happened to him relate to you?

   Possible Answers: Clare became excited. He couldn't wait to share what he was learning with other people and explore new possibilities. Gradually he found it easier to make important life decisions in light of his new-found faith. Over time, God changed the desires of Clare's heart, and after three years, he sold his business. [Note: It's important to let participants know that the halftime process can take weeks, months, even years.] Allow participants to share the ways in which Clare's experience impacts them—inspires, challenges, frightens, etc.

 3. Bob Buford knows about the risks of wrestling with the possibilities for significance. He observes, "In tossing aside the security blanket that keeps you safe and warm, you may have to set aside some

VIDEO HIGHLIGHTS

1. What role did Clare's view of God play in his journey from success to significance?

2. Once Clare got a taste of what it meant to allow God to guide his life, how did he respond? How might what happened to him relate to you?

3. Bob Buford knows about the risks of wrestling with the possibilities for significance. He observes, "In tossing aside the security blanket that keeps you safe and warm, you may have to set aside some familiar markers and reference points. You may feel, at least at first, that you're losing control of your life. To which I say, 'Good for you!'" What do you think he meant by this comment?

4. Clare views the activities of his second half as having eternal significance. What things do you view as having eternal significance?

HALFTIME CLIP

There will always be reasons to stay where you are. It is faith that calls you to move on. —**BOB BUFORD**

PLANNING NOTES

familiar markers and reference points. You may feel, at least at first, that you're losing control of your life. To which I say, 'Good for you!'" What do you think he meant by this comment?

Possible Answers: It's easy to coast and keep doing the same things the same ways. When we step out of our comfort zones, we may feel afraid because we don't seem to have as much control. But that's okay because God is in control. When we relinquish control of our lives to God, he will take care of us. We must relinquish control in order to take the next steps on the journey toward significance. We can't hold back and go forward; we have to choose one or the other.

 4. Clare views the activities of his second half as having eternal significance. What things do you view as having eternal significance?

Possible Answers: Encourage participants to explore and share a number of things that have eternal significance. These may include using the arts to communicate the message of Jesus Christ, taking a public stand on Bible-related issues, leading people to Jesus Christ, sharing Jesus' love with other people, doing what God calls us to do through faithful obedience at our workplaces, taking a second vocation that allows us to use our talents and abilities, visiting prisoners, etc.

HALFTIME CLIP

> *There will always be reasons to stay where you are. It is faith that calls you to move on.*
> **—BOB BUFORD**

HALFTIME PERSPECTIVE

It's Time to Chart a New Course

- It may come on slowly—or almost demand to be addressed.
- It's about "a time to search and a time to give up" (Ecclesiastes 3:6).
- It's a time to search for new horizons and take on new challenges.
- It's a time to give up regrets.
- It's a time to start living by your own epitaph, perhaps daring to believe that what you ultimately leave behind will be more important than anything you could have possessed during your lifetime.
- It's a time to take risks because that's where the game is won or lost.
- It's about releasing the seeds of creativity and energy that have been implanted within you.

SESSION FOUR: Game Plan for Significance   85

4. Clare views the activities of his second half as having eternal significance. What things do you view as having eternal significance?

HALFTIME CLIP

There will always be reasons to stay where you are. It is faith that calls you to move on. —**BOB BUFORD**

---

84   HALFTIME PARTICIPANT'S GUIDE

HALFTIME PERSPECTIVE

It's Time to Chart a New Course

- It may come on slowly—or almost demand to be addressed.
- It's about "a time to search and a time to give up" (Ecclesiastes 3:6).
- It's a time to search for new horizons and take on new challenges.
- It's a time to give up regrets.
- It's a time to start living by your own epitaph, perhaps daring to believe that what you ultimately leave behind will be more important than anything you could have possessed during your lifetime.
- It's a time to take risks because that's where the game is won or lost.
- It's about releasing the seeds of creativity and energy that have been implanted within you.
- It's about identifying yourself by internal standards—your character, your values, your beliefs, your contributions, your mission—rather than by your work, your possessions, your busyness, your children.
- It's about investing yourself in service to other people—and receiving the personal joy that comes as a result of that investment.
- It's about developing a mind-set, an inner compass, that is fixed on the things that define your true self as God has created you.

PLANNING NOTES

- It's about identifying yourself by internal standards—your character, your values, your beliefs, your contributions, your mission—rather than by your work, your possessions, your busyness, your children.
- It's about investing yourself in service to other people—and receiving the personal joy that comes as a result of that investment.
- It's about developing a mind-set, an inner compass, that is fixed on the things that define your true self as God has created you.

Large Group Exploration (8 minutes)

Developing a Personal Mission Statement

Perhaps you have already discovered what's in your box and feel enthusiastic about the opportunities for significance that you never dreamed existed. But it is not enough to feel like doing something significant. The newly discovered resolve that comes when you place just one thing into the box will fade if you don't apply it to a related goal. The time for good intentions is passed. It's time for each of us to develop a personal mission statement.

A personal mission statement defines what is most important to us and how we will arrange our priorities. It will help each of us define how we want our lives to count—what we will do and how we will go about doing it. It will release us to be ourselves and effectively use the gifts and talents we already possess.

 1. What did you think or feel when you read or heard the words *personal mission statement?* Why?

Possible Answers: Encourage participants to express their excitement and intimidation about the prospect of writing a personal mission statement. It's a much easier process when our fears and objections are brought into the light! Some participants may think that writing a personal mission statement is difficult; view it as something they do in the business world, but not in their personal world; wonder how to go about writing one; feel excited about discovering and expressing their personal mission; hope their spouse will agree with what they come up with.

 2. What has been your previous experience with mission statements? Have you ever had a personal mission statement? If so, what did it accomplish for you? What do you see as the limitations or drawbacks of a mission statement?

Possible Answers: Encourage participants to share their experiences with the group. Encourage them to be specific, such as describing a time when focusing on their mission kept them from pursuing a direction that they or

SESSION FOUR: Game Plan for Significance   **85**

LARGE GROUP EXPLORATION

Developing a Personal Mission Statement

Perhaps you have already discovered what's in your box and feel enthusiastic about the opportunities for significance that you never dreamed existed. But it is not enough to feel like doing something significant. The newly discovered resolve that comes when you place just one thing into the box will fade if you don't apply it to a related goal. The time for good intentions is passed. It's time for each of us to develop a personal mission statement.

A personal mission statement defines what is most important to us and how we will arrange our priorities. It will help each of us define how we want our lives to count—what we will do and how we will go about doing it. It will release us to be ourselves and effectively use the gifts and talents we already possess.

1. What did you think or feel when you read or heard the words *personal mission statement?* Why?

2. What has been your previous experience with mission statements? Have you ever had a personal mission statement? If so, what did it accomplish for you? What do you see as the limitations or drawbacks of a mission statement?

PLANNING NOTES

their company were not equipped to handle. Some participants may have had experience in rewriting an obsolete mission statement. The point is to help participants recognize the importance of developing a personal mission statement and to have appropriate expectations for it.

 3. Stephen Covey, author of *The Seven Habits of Highly Effective People,* suggests that when we develop a personal mission statement, we should focus on what we wish to be and do, based on the values and principles that undergird our beliefs and actions. What might some of the benefits be of approaching a mission statement this way as opposed to using other criteria?

Possible Answers: These will vary but may include developing personal mission statements that reflect our uniqueness, be challenged to be honest with ourselves about what we believe and who we are, link our personal mission statements to what we've each put into our box, have personal mission statements that will endure over time, etc.

 4. Read the parable of the talents in Matthew 25:14–30. Bob Buford says, "The wonderful message from this story is that you and I will be held accountable only for what we were given, not for what others might have or expect from us. The guy who was given only two talents and doubled them was esteemed as highly as the guy who started out with five. We are not all given the same equipment, but we are expected to know what we were given and find ways to invest ourselves wisely."

In what ways do you think developing a personal mission statement guides us in being better stewards of the talents God has given us?

Possible Answers: The process of developing a personal mission statement will cause us to identify our talents, our uniqueness, and our passions. Once we have developed our personal mission statements, we can be more focused in what we do. Furthermore, a mission statement will aid us in planning new directions, provide hope as we start making necessary changes, and provide a concrete reminder of the commitments we have made.

3. Stephen Covey, author of *The Seven Habits of Highly Effective People,* suggests that when we develop a personal mission statement, we should focus on what we wish to be and do, based on the values and principles that undergird our beliefs and actions. What might some of the benefits be of approaching a mission statement this way as opposed to using other criteria?

4. Read the parable of the talents in Matthew 25:14–30. Bob Buford says, "The wonderful message from this story is that you and I will be held accountable only for what we were given, not for what others might have or expect from us. The guy who was given only two talents and doubled them was esteemed as highly as the guy who started out with five. We are not all given the same equipment, but we are expected to know what we were given and find ways to invest ourselves wisely."

In what ways do you think developing a personal mission statement guides us in being better stewards of the talents God has given us?

PLANNING NOTES

Pause for Personal Reflection

What we've covered during the previous sessions has prepared us for taking action—for developing a personal mission statement. Now it's time to pause to reflect on what needs to go into that statement. (We will begin writing our personal mission statements at the end of this session.)

HALFTIME TIP

Peter Drucker suggests two important questions to help you discover the unique role God has prepared you to play:

1. What have you achieved? (This has to do with your competence.)
2. What do you care deeply about? (This has to do with your passion.)

If you look deeply enough inside yourself and are honest about combining your competence with your passion, you will find the mission that is best suited to you.

- Write down several things I can do that are uniquely me, ambitious, and have a degree of risk.
- In which would I like to make a real difference?
- Which things have I done uncommonly well?
- I probably have twenty-five or more productive years ahead of me. How do I want to spend them?
- If I could accomplish nothing else, what are the top five things of significance I want to do before I die?

Let participants know when there is one minute remaining. You may also want to tell participants that writing a personal mission statement is rarely a ten-minute task. Suggest that those who find it difficult to work on this exercise make the extra effort to go through the Halftime Perspective: Tips for Choosing Your Life Mission (page 89). Some of the steps that are helpful in identifying a life mission may be helpful in developing a personal mission statement as well.

Pause for Personal Reflection

What we've covered during the previous sessions has prepared us for taking action—for developing a personal mission statement. Now it's time to pause to reflect on what needs to go into that statement.

HALFTIME TIP

Peter Drucker suggests two important questions to help you discover the unique role God has prepared you to play:

1. What have you achieved? (This has to do with your competence.)

2. What do you care deeply about? (This has to do with your passion.)

If you look deeply enough inside yourself and are honest about combining your competence with your passion, you will find the mission that is best suited to you.

Write down several things I can do that are uniquely me, ambitious, and have a degree of risk.

In which would I like to make a real difference?

Which things have I done uncommonly well?

I probably have twenty-five or more productive years ahead of me. How do I want to spend them?

If I could accomplish nothing else, what are the top five things of significance I want to do before I die?

HALFTIME PERSPECTIVE

Tips for Choosing Your Life Mission

In addition to writing a personal mission statement, the halftime process involves choosing a life mission—usually selecting a specific task, cause, or organization—on which you will focus much of your time, talents, and resources during your second half. The following tips will help you begin pinpointing what your life mission will be.

1. Recognize how far you've already come in your journey toward significance. A key part of identifying your life mission is knowing who you are—your strengths, weaknesses,

PLANNING NOTES

HALFTIME PERSPECTIVE

Tips for Choosing Your Life Mission

In addition to writing a personal mission statement, the halftime process involves choosing a life mission—usually selecting a specific task, cause, or organization—on which you will focus much of your time, talents, and resources during your second half. The following tips will help you begin pinpointing what your life mission will be.

1. Recognize how far you've already come in your journey toward significance. A key part of identifying your life mission is knowing who you are—your strengths, weaknesses, aspirations, regrets, hopes, gifts. You already know what you have been given. Now it's time to find ways to invest yourself wisely.

2. Be patient with yourself. It will take time to work through your issues and plans. Don't jump into your life mission too fast. At the same time, don't be too patient to take the plunge.

3. Don't waste time and energy fantasizing about things that will never happen. Instead, face the tough questions so you can discover the real you.

4. Make lists of things you want to do—things to which you are committed, slogans and creeds that reflect the true you, statements that combine what you believe with what you want to do.

5. Seek out reliable counsel—trustworthy people with whom you can dialogue about your ideas. Ask them how they see you. Listen carefully to what they say and resist the temptation to be defensive. They can provide a fresh perspective on who you are and how God might use you during your second half.

6. Keep a journal as you seek your second-half mission. It will help you remember where you've been and clarify where you are headed. Writing out your thoughts also gives you the opportunity to see them on paper, where you can more easily review and evaluate them.

7. Prayer is a significant part of the halftime process. Psalm 139:23–24 reads, "Search me, O God, and know my heart; test me and know my anxious thoughts. See if there is any offensive way in me, and lead me in the way everlasting." God wants to help each of us examine our path and guide us toward our calling. He does not waste what he has built. He didn't create you with specialized abilities and your unique temperament for no reason. God desires for you to serve him just by being who you are.

8. Before drilling for oil, an investor does seismic testing to see what an area may produce. Likewise, do your own seismic testing to get a little hands-on experience in something you may want to pursue. For example, assist

continued on page 146...

aspirations, regrets, hopes, gifts. You already know what you have been given. Now it's time to find ways to invest yourself wisely.

2. Be patient with yourself. It will take time to work through your issues and plans. Don't jump into your life mission too fast. At the same time, don't be too patient to take the plunge.

3. Don't waste time and energy fantasizing about things that will never happen. Instead, face the tough questions so you can discover the real you.

4. Make lists of things you want to do—things to which you are committed, slogans and creeds that reflect the true you, statements that combine what you believe with what you want to do.

5. Seek out reliable counsel—trustworthy people with whom you can dialogue about your ideas. Ask them how they see you. Listen carefully to what they say and resist the temptation to be defensive. They can provide a fresh perspective on who you are and how God might use you during your second half.

6. Keep a journal as you seek your second-half mission. It will help you remember where you've been and clarify where you are headed. Writing out your thoughts also gives you the opportunity to see them on paper, where you can more easily review and evaluate them.

7. Prayer is a significant part of the halftime process. Psalm 139:23–24 reads, "Search me, O God, and know my heart; test me and know my anxious thoughts. See if there is any offensive way in me, and lead me in the way everlasting." God wants to help each of us examine our path and guide us toward our calling. He does not waste what he has built.

Continued on next page…

He didn't create you with specialized abilities and your unique temperament for no reason. God desires for you to serve him just by being who you are.

8. Before drilling for oil, an investor does seismic testing to see what an area may produce. Likewise, do your own seismic testing to get a little hands-on experience in something you may want to pursue. For example, assist someone in doing what you might like to do during your second half. Or take a short-term assignment. Or organize a focus group of people who are involved in your field of interest and ask them questions. If the exploratory results are negative, keep evaluating. You're saving yourself lots of trouble, expense, and time.

9. Consider doing what you currently do differently. Could you work fewer hours and invest yourself in a life mission that matters? Do you need to begin moving in a completely new direction? Are you ready to begin a parallel career?

10. Relax. Remember, what you do best for God will rise out of your core being—what God has created within you.

HALFTIME CLIP

I couldn't figure out why God would equip me as an entrepreneur, conceiver, starter, team builder, manager, and leader and then put me someplace where those things are worthless. I was relieved to discover that God does not waste what he has built. I am the same me I was in the first half, only applied to a different venue.   **—BOB BUFORD**

PLANNING NOTES

someone in doing what you might like to do during your second half. Or take a short-term assignment. Or organize a focus group of people who are involved in your field of interest and ask them questions. If the exploratory results are negative, keep evaluating. You're saving yourself lots of trouble, expense, and time.

9. Consider doing what you currently do differently. Could you work fewer hours and invest yourself in a life mission that matters? Do you need to begin moving in a completely new direction? Are you ready to begin a parallel career?

10. Relax. Remember, what you do best for God will rise out of your core being—what God has created within you.

HALFTIME CLIP

I couldn't figure out why God would equip me as an entrepreneur, conceiver, starter, team builder, manager, and leader and then put me someplace where those things are worthless. I was relieved to discover that God does not waste what he has built. I am the same me I was in the first half, only applied to a different venue.
                                        —BOB BUFORD

Small Group Exploration (8 minutes)

Clearing the Plate

Each of us has been taking steps that will lead toward significance. We have thought about many aspects of our lives and had to wrestle with challenging topics. Yet another part of the halftime process involves weeding out time- and energy-consuming activities that seem to control us but are not taking us where we want (and need) to go.

Unfortunately, many things—even good things—conspire to keep us where we've been and hinder our halftime journey. Thus it is important for us to recapture the majority of our time so we can use a portion of our time, talent, and treasure in discovering and pursuing our second-half mission.

 1. In his parable about the farmer sowing seeds, Jesus shared truths that we can apply to halftime. Let's read Matthew 13:3–9 and think of ourselves—our lives, our dreams, our goals—as seeds that have the opportunity to grow and be fruitful.

He didn't create you with specialized abilities and your unique temperament for no reason. God desires for you to serve him just by being who you are.

8. Before drilling for oil, an investor does seismic testing to see what an area may produce. Likewise, do your own seismic testing to get a little hands-on experience in something you may want to pursue. For example, assist someone in doing what you might like to do during your second half. Or take a short-term assignment. Or organize a focus group of people who are involved in your field of interest and ask them questions. If the exploratory results are negative, keep evaluating. You're saving yourself lots of trouble, expense, and time.

9. Consider doing what you currently do differently. Could you work fewer hours and invest yourself in a life mission that matters? Do you need to begin moving in a completely new direction? Are you ready to begin a parallel career?

10. Relax. Remember, what you do best for God will rise out of your core being—what God has created within you.

HALFTIME CLIP

I couldn't figure out why God would equip me as an entrepreneur, conceiver, starter, team builder, manager, and leader and then put me someplace where those things are worthless. I was relieved to discover that God does not waste what he has built. I am the same me I was in the first half, only applied to a different venue.
—BOB BUFORD

SMALL GROUP EXPLORATION

Clearing the Plate

Each of us has been taking steps that will lead toward significance. We have thought about many aspects of our lives and had to wrestle with challenging topics. Yet another part of the halftime process involves weeding out time- and energy-consuming activities that seem to control us but are not taking us where we want (and need) to go.

Unfortunately, many things—even good things—conspire to keep us where we've been and hinder our halftime journey. Thus it is important for us to recapture the majority of our time so we can use a portion of our time, talent, and treasure in discovering and pursuing our second-half mission.

1. In his parable about the farmer sowing seeds, Jesus shared truths that we can apply to halftime. Let's read Matthew 13:3–9 and think of ourselves—our lives, our dreams, our goals—as seeds that have the opportunity to grow and be fruitful.

   a. What kind of crop resulted from the seeds that fell onto good soil? What parallels might there be to our lives, to the impact each of us can have if we nurture what God has given us—our talents, resources, abilities?

   b. What things in life can scatter our potential in rocky places where there is little nourishment or choke out our innermost dreams and desires?

---

a. What kind of crop resulted from the seeds that fell onto good soil? What parallels might there be to our lives, to the impact each of us can have if we nurture what God has given us—our talents, resources, abilities?

Possible Answers: The seeds that fell onto good soil produced a good crop, multiplying many times over. Each of us also has the potential to use the seeds of our lives to make a difference. [Note: Emphasize that each of us can cultivate what we've been given—our talents, gifts, resources. We don't have to be rich or have lots of opportunities in order to find significance and make a positive impact in people's lives.]

b. What things in life can scatter our potential in rocky places where there is little nourishment or choke out our innermost dreams and desires?

Possible Answers: These will vary greatly. Encourage participants to consider the range of activities and commitments that have the ability to scatter our potential as well as the relationships and attitudes that hold us back and choke out our vision.

 2. As a result of his spiritual commitment, Clare DeGraaf began learning about the Christian faith. He tested the waters of his future mission by sharing what he had learned with others. What big distraction did he need to clear out of his life in order to progress toward significance? What is involved in making that kind of commitment?

Possible Answers: Clare came to a point where he needed to sell his business. What is amazing about this is that his management staff recognized that Clare's heart was no longer in the business. They were the ones who told him what needed to change, which Clare knew was true. To make this kind of commitment, you have to be sold out to your personal mission.

 3. Bob Buford believes that each of us has social capital—time, money, and knowledge—that is available to reinvest or spend in the community that nurtures us. In what ways do you think our busy lives crowd out opportunities to share what God has given us?

Possible Answers: It's easy to become focused on our jobs, families, and recreational interests and lose sight of the world around us. True service to others isn't the first thing on many people's minds. Expending our social capital doesn't necessarily bring recognition or reward from others. Yet when we expend our social capital for the benefit of other people, we receive much in return.

SMALL GROUP EXPLORATION

Clearing the Plate

Each of us has been taking steps that will lead toward significance. We have thought about many aspects of our lives and had to wrestle with challenging topics. Yet another part of the halftime process involves weeding out time- and energy-consuming activities that seem to control us but are not taking us where we want (and need) to go.

Unfortunately, many things—even good things—conspire to keep us where we've been and hinder our halftime journey. Thus it is important for us to recapture the majority of our time so we can use a portion of our time, talent, and treasure in discovering and pursuing our second-half mission.

1. In his parable about the farmer sowing seeds, Jesus shared truths that we can apply to halftime. Let's read Matthew 13:3–9 and think of ourselves—our lives, our dreams, our goals—as seeds that have the opportunity to grow and be fruitful.

   a. What kind of crop resulted from the seeds that fell onto good soil? What parallels might there be to our lives, to the impact each of us can have if we nurture what God has given us—our talents, resources, abilities?

   b. What things in life can scatter our potential in rocky places where there is little nourishment or choke out our innermost dreams and desires?

2. As a result of his spiritual commitment, Clare DeGraaf began learning about the Christian faith. He tested the waters of his future mission by sharing what he had learned with others. What big distraction did he need to clear out of his life in order to progress toward significance? What is involved in making that kind of commitment?

3. Bob Buford believes that each of us has social capital—time, money, and knowledge—that is available to reinvest or spend in the community that nurtures us. In what ways do you think our busy lives crowd out opportunities to share what God has given us?

4. A key element of the second half involves regaining control of our lives—calling our own shots. What are some reasons why it's important for each of us to slow down, return to the core of who we are, and recapture the majority of our time and other resources?

PLANNING NOTES

4. A key element of the second half involves regaining control of our lives—calling our own shots. What are some reasons why it's important for each of us to slow down, return to the core of who we are, and recapture the majority of our time and other resources?

Possible Answers: Until we slow down, we won't have time to think about who we are and the direction in which we should proceed. We will keep spinning too fast, and important things—including key relationships—will suffer. It takes time to explore the application and ramifications of our halftime options. We need to recapture the majority of our time so we will have a portion of the time, talent, and treasure God has given us to put toward fulfilling our life mission. Otherwise, we'll continue to be frustrated by unfulfilled dreams and desires.

HALFTIME CLIP

Desire alone will not allow you to do something new in your second half; you must create the capacity to do it. If you are being controlled by too many time- and energy-consuming activities, you will continue to be frustrated by unfulfilled dreams and desires.

—BOB BUFORD

Pause for Personal Reflection

Now it's time to pause to consider how we will spend our time and resources in light of who we are, what's in our respective boxes, and our personal mission statements.

- How willing am I:

  to consider how I spend my time?
  to determine which things need to have a higher priority and which things I can do less often or perhaps not at all?
  to make the necessary changes?

- What are the relationships and activities in my life that demand my attention and compete for priority? Which of these may be keeping me from wrestling with who I am, what I profess to believe about my life, and what I can do to bring meaning and significance to my life?

- If I were to reorder my time and priorities, rethink my vision of what life could be, look leisurely into the holiest chamber of my heart, and respond to my soul's deepest longings, what would my life be like? Where would I spend my time? What would I have to clear out of my life?

2. As a result of his spiritual commitment, Clare DeGraaf began learning about the Christian faith. He tested the waters of his future mission by sharing what he had learned with others. What big distraction did he need to clear out of his life in order to progress toward significance? What is involved in making that kind of commitment?

3. Bob Buford believes that each of us has social capital—time, money, and knowledge—that is available to reinvest or spend in the community that nurtures us. In what ways do you think our busy lives crowd out opportunities to share what God has given us?

4. A key element of the second half involves regaining control of our lives—calling our own shots. What are some reasons why it's important for each of us to slow down, return to the core of who we are, and recapture the majority of our time and other resources?

PLANNING NOTES

HALFTIME CLIP

Desire alone will not allow you to do something new in your second half; you must create the capacity to do it. If you are being controlled by too many time- and energy-consuming activities, you will continue to be frustrated by unfulfilled dreams and desires.

—BOB BUFORD

Pause for Personal Reflection
Now it's time to pause to consider how we will spend our time and resources in light of who we are, what's in our respective boxes, and our personal mission statements.

How willing am I:
- to consider how I spend my time?
- to determine which things need to have a higher priority and which things I can do less often or perhaps not at all?
- to make the necessary changes?

What are the relationships and activities in my life that demand my attention and compete for priority? Which of these may be keeping me from wrestling with who I am, what I profess to believe about my life, and what I can do to bring meaning and significance to my life?

If I were to reorder my time and priorities, rethink my vision of what life could be, look leisurely into the holiest chamber of my heart, and respond to my soul's deepest longings, what would my life be like? Where would I spend my time? What would I have to clear out of my life?

HALFTIME CLIP

Once we return to the core—once we know who we are and what's in the box—we can accept the fact that some of the things on the perimeter of our lives will not receive as much attention as they once did. Some things will be more important than others; some may need to be ignored altogether. But regardless of what stays and what gets tossed aside, the point is that we no longer let someone else decide that for us. We create the capacity for the things that matter.

—BOB BUFORD

> Let participants know when there is one minute remaining.

HALFTIME CLIP

Once we return to the core—once we know who we are and what's in the box—we can accept the fact that some of the things on the perimeter of our lives will not receive as much attention as they once did. Some things will be more important than others; some may need to be ignored altogether. But regardless of what stays and what gets tossed aside, the point is that we no longer let someone else decide that for us. We create the capacity for the things that matter.   **—BOB BUFORD**

HALFTIME DRILL

Time Priority Checklist

Once we identify the mainspring of our attitudes, beliefs, and actions and determine what should be in our personal mission statement, our best intentions to live a significant life may become buried beneath too many time- and energy-consuming activities.

Read the following checklist and start reassessing each priority in light of your halftime decisions and commitments. Write out the specific aspects of any priorities that you need to prune or to which you need to devote more time and energy.

Note: Pruning some priorities and nurturing others is a dynamic process. You may want to go through this checklist several times as you go through the halftime process. Your assessment is likely to be different every time.

Priority	Prune	Develop
Knowing God through a personal relationship with Jesus Christ		
Spending time with family members		
Developing friendships		
Hours I spend at or thinking about work		
Things on which I focus my mind		

continued on page 154...

If I were to reorder my time and priorities, rethink my vision of what life could be, look leisurely into the holiest chamber of my heart, and respond to my soul's deepest longings, what would my life be like? Where would I spend my time? What would I have to clear out of my life?

HALFTIME CLIP

Once we return to the core—once we know who we are and what's in the box—we can accept the fact that some of the things on the perimeter of our lives will not receive as much attention as they once did. Some things will be more important than others; some may need to be ignored altogether. But regardless of what stays and what gets tossed aside, the point is that we no longer let someone else decide that for us. We create the capacity for the things that matter.

—BOB BUFORD

HALFTIME DRILL

Time Priority Checklist

Once we identify the mainspring of our attitudes, beliefs, and actions and determine what should be in our personal mission statement, our best intentions to live a significant life may become buried beneath too many time- and energy-consuming activities.

Read the following checklist and start reassessing each priority in light of your halftime decisions and commitments. Write out the specific aspects of any priorities that you need to prune or to which you need to devote more time and energy.

Note: Pruning some priorities and nurturing others is a dynamic process. You may want to go through this checklist several times as you go through the halftime process. Your assessment is likely to be different every time.

Priority	Prune	Develop
Knowing God through a personal relationship with Jesus Christ		
Spending time with family members		
Developing friendships		
Hours I spend at or thinking about work		
Things on which I focus my mind		
Recreational activities		

Continued on next page...

PLANNING NOTES

Recreational activities		
Reading		
Praying		
Exercising		
Thinking about my life-related possibilities		
Forgiving myself and asking for God's forgiveness		
Assessing my strengths and weaknesses		
Taking time to dream about what could be		
Asking God for wisdom and strength		
Applying God's promises to my life		
Assessing my talents and treasures		
Thinking about my uniqueness		
Thinking about ways in which I could make an eternal difference		

HALFTIME DRILL

Time Priority Checklist

Once we identify the mainspring of our attitudes, beliefs, and actions and determine what should be in our personal mission statement, our best intentions to live a significant life may become buried beneath too many time- and energy-consuming activities.

Read the following checklist and start reassessing each priority in light of your halftime decisions and commitments. Write out the specific aspects of any priorities that you need to prune or to which you need to devote more time and energy.

Note: Pruning some priorities and nurturing others is a dynamic process. You may want to go through this checklist several times as you go through the halftime process. Your assessment is likely to be different every time.

Priority	Prune	Develop
Knowing God through a personal relationship with Jesus Christ		
Spending time with family members		
Developing friendships		
Hours I spend at or thinking about work		
Things on which I focus my mind		
Recreational activities		

Continued on next page . . .

Reading		
Praying		
Exercising		
Thinking about my life-related possibilities		
Forgiving myself and asking for God's forgiveness		
Assessing my strengths and weaknesses		
Taking time to dream about what could be		
Asking God for wisdom and strength		
Applying God's promises to my life		
Assessing my talents and treasures		
Thinking about my uniqueness		
Thinking about ways in which I could make an eternal difference		

PLANNING NOTES

Group Discussion (6 minutes)

Now it's time to wrap up our discovery time.

> Give participants a moment to transition from their thoughtfulness and begin sharing their observations with the entire group. Use the following questions as discussion starters.

 1. Clare mentioned how God had changed the desires of his heart from loving business to loving ministry. In what ways has God been changing your heart since we started this series?

 2. Learning new things is essential as we seek to take control of our lives in light of God's calling for us.

   a. What are some of the benefits of continuing to learn and acting on what we learn during the second half of our lives?

   b. Describe some ways in which we can keep on learning during the second half of our lives.

 3. As it turned out, Clare's expertise in business prepared him to do exactly what God wanted him to do. In what ways is this an encouragement to you as you face the future?

HALFTIME CLIP

> *The feeling of being hurried is not usually the result of living a full life and having no time. It is, on the contrary, born of a vague fear that we are wasting our life. When we do not do the one thing we ought to do, we have no time for anything else—we are the busiest people in the world.*
>
> **—ERIC HOFFER**

GROUP DISCUSSION

1. Clare mentioned how God had changed the desires of his heart from loving business to loving ministry. In what ways has God been changing your heart since we started this series?

2. Learning new things is essential as we seek to take control of our lives in light of God's calling for us.

   a. What are some of the benefits of continuing to learn and acting on what we learn during the second half of our lives?

   b. Describe some ways in which we can keep on learning during the second half of our lives.

3. As it turned out, Clare's expertise in business prepared him to do exactly what God wanted him to do. In what ways is this an encouragement to you as you face the future?

HALFTIME CLIP

The feeling of being hurried is not usually the result of living a full life and having no time. It is, on the contrary, born of a vague fear that we are wasting our life. When we do not do the one thing we ought to do, we have no time for anything else—we are the busiest people in the world.
—ERIC HOFFER

PLANNING NOTES

ACTION POINTS

minutes

> The following points are reproduced on page 99 of the Participant's Guide.

I'd like to take a moment to summarize the key points we explored today. After I have reviewed these points, I will give you a moment to consider what you will commit to do as a result of what you have discovered during this session.

> Read the following points and pause afterward so participants can consider and write out their commitments.

 1. Defining what's in our box is an important step in the journey from success to significance. But unless our mission matches our intention, we will experience a dissonance that ultimately will be destructive. So it is essential that we each choose a mission and formulate a personal mission statement that matches whatever we put into our box. Once we have formulated our mission statement, we can begin to establish a game plan that will lead us in the direction we want to go.

If you are ready to do so, write out your mission statement. Even if you are unsure of what it should be, at least write a proposed mission statement. Then set it aside for at least a week and follow the steps in the Halftime Drill below.

HALFTIME DRILL

Writing Your Mission Statement
Make lists of things to do during your second half, things you are committed to, slogans and creeds that reflect the true you, statements that combine what you believe with what you want to do with the rest of your life. After you have made your lists, pray. Read what you have written. Reflect. Listen. Share what you have written with your spouse and a small group of friends. Then put the paper away in a drawer. Pray some more. Listen a lot. Think about what you love to do the most, and let these thoughts roll gently through your soul like lazy waves on the ocean. After a week (or longer), write your mission statement.

ACTION POINTS

What will you commit to do as a result of what you have discovered during this session?

1. Defining what's in our box is an important step in the journey from success to significance. But unless our mission matches our intention, we will experience a dissonance that ultimately will be destructive. So it is essential that we each choose a mission and formulate a personal mission statement that matches whatever we put into our box. Once we have formulated our mission statement, we can begin to establish a game plan that will lead us in the direction we want to go.

   If you are ready to do so, write out your mission statement. Even if you are unsure of what it should be, at least write a proposed mission statement. Then set it aside for at least a week and follow the steps in the Halftime Drill below.

HALFTIME DRILL

Writing Your Mission Statement
Make lists of things to do during your second half, things you are committed to, slogans and creeds that reflect the true you, statements that combine what you believe with what you want to do with the rest of your life. After you have made your lists, pray. Read what you have written. Reflect. Listen. Share what you have written with your spouse and a small group of friends. Then put the paper away in a drawer. Pray some more. Listen a lot. Think about what you love to do the most, and let these thoughts roll gently through your soul like lazy waves on the ocean. After a week (or longer), write your mission statement.

PLANNING NOTES

2. We don't have to live life with regrets. Instead of just staying where we are and being afraid of change, each of us—no matter what our background may be—can take risks and step toward significance. We can clear our plate of distractions and unnecessary demands and start living out our personal life missions. We can embark on the journey of doing the good works God has ordained for us to do.

Now that you've written your proposed personal mission statement, how would you define your life mission?

Note: It should fit within your mission statement, and Bob Buford recommends that it be something ambitious that also has a degree of risk to it. When the odds are big and the task is demanding, you'll be drawn to contribute your best and release energies you didn't know you had.

Set aside several hours this week to think about:

- **The risks you may need to take.**
- **The changes you need to make to clear your plate of distractions.**
- **What you need to learn in order to keep moving toward significance.**

So you can begin living out your life mission.

CLOSING MEDITATION

minute

Dear God, thank you for giving us the opportunity to explore who you have made us to be and what it is you have for us to do. It's exciting to start writing out our personal mission statements and thinking about our life missions. But it's also a new journey for us, one we're not sure about, one that reminds us how much we need you. Please help us to remember that you love us and are willing to give us wisdom as we seek to fulfill your calling for us. Give us the courage to continue this halftime process, to realize the joys and rewards of living a significant second half. Thank you that you are with us as we undertake this journey. Amen.

2. We don't have to live life with regrets. Instead of just staying where we are and being afraid of change, each of us—no matter what our background may be—can take risks and step toward significance. We can clear our plate of distractions and unnecessary demands and start living out our personal life missions. We can embark on the journey of doing the good works God has ordained for us to do.

Now that you've written your proposed personal mission statement, how would you define your life mission?

Note: It should fit within your mission statement, and Bob Buford recommends that it be something ambitious that also has a degree of risk to it. When the odds are big and the task is demanding, you'll be drawn to contribute your best and release energies you didn't know you had.

Set aside several hours this week to think about:
- The risks you may need to take.
- The changes you need to make to clear your plate of distractions.
- What you need to learn in order to keep moving toward significance.

So you can begin living out your life mission.

PLANNING NOTES

Mission Statements

Many businesses and other organizations have developed mission statements, vision statements, or credos that attempt to explain why the company or organization exists and what it hopes to accomplish. When such declarations are well stated, they are usually easily understood and very simple. A mission statement becomes, as a team of consultants once noted in the *Harvard Business Review*, "the magnetic North Pole, the focal point" for that business. Everything the company or organization does points in that direction.

Developing a personal mission statement makes a lot of sense. In fact, you will not get very far in your second half without knowing your life mission. Can your mission be stated in a sentence or two?

A good way to begin formulating a mission statement is with some questions (and honest answers).

- What is your passion?
- What have you achieved?
- What have you done uncommonly well?
- How are you wired?
- Where do you belong?
- What are the "shoulds" that have trailed you during the first half?

These and other questions like them will direct you toward the self your heart longs for; they will help you discover the task for which you were especially made.

HALFTIME CLIP

My life mission is: To transform the latent energy in American Christianity into active energy.

This is what I do; it is how I want my life to count. It releases me to be myself—to use gifts that are already there. I do not have to become something that feels uncomfortable or strange. If your own mission statement fits you as well, it will be the right one for you. If it forces you into something that does not fit, it will be someone else's mission. **—BOB BUFORD**

HALFTIME PERSPECTIVE

Mission Statements

Many businesses and other organizations have developed mission statements, vision statements, or credos that attempt to explain why the company or organization exists and what it hopes to accomplish. When such declarations are well stated, they are usually easily understood and very simple. A mission statement becomes, as a team of consultants once noted in the *Harvard Business Review,* "the magnetic North Pole, the focal point" for that business. Everything the company or organization does points in that direction.

Developing a personal mission statement makes a lot of sense. In fact, you will not get very far in your second half without knowing your life mission. Can your mission be stated in a sentence or two?

A good way to begin formulating a mission statement is with some questions (and honest answers).

- What is your passion?
- What have you achieved?
- What have you done uncommonly well?
- How are you wired?
- Where do you belong?
- What are the "shoulds" that have trailed you during the first half?

These and other questions like them will direct you toward the self your heart longs for; they will help you discover the task for which you were especially made.

HALFTIME CLIP

My life mission is: To transform the latent energy in American Christianity into active energy.

This is what I do; it is how I want my life to count. It releases me to be myself—to use gifts that are already there. I do not have to become something that feels uncomfortable or strange. If your own mission statement fits you as well, it will be the right one for you. If it forces you into something that does not fit, it will be someone else's mission.

—BOB BUFORD

PLANNING NOTES

5

The Best of Your Years

BEFORE YOU LEAD

Synopsis

The final video segment of this series features people from various walks of life who, through the process of halftime, gave themselves permission to pursue significance—God's calling for each of them. As a result, their second-half years are becoming the best years of their lives. They have discovered a deeper relationship with God and are living lives of significance as they put their faith into action. They are passionate and excited about life. And they are making a difference in their world as a new quality of life unfolds before them.

In addition to the people you have already met through this video series, you'll meet:

- Doug Mazza, former COO of the Hyundai Corporation, whom God guided into a new ministry.
- Dr. Joe McIlhaney, an obstetrician-gynecologist who started the Medical Institute for Sexual Health, which creates medically reliable materials and resources relating to abstinence and sexual health.
- Cynthia Gonzales, who was offered early retirement from her employer and found a new calling.

This session focuses on the quality of life possible during one's second half. Participants will discover the importance of serving people, controlling their inner experiences, and continuing to learn and grow as they seek to make the rest of their years the best of their years.

Building on the previous *Halftime* sessions, this session will guide participants in discovering the blessedness that comes when they have a dynamic, personal relationship with God through Jesus Christ and use their God-given gifts to serve other people. This emphasis may stimulate participants to want to know more about God and the Bible.

Psychologist Mihaly Csikszentmihalyi, who is mentioned in Bob Buford's book *Halftime,* spent twenty-five years trying to figure out what makes people happy. He discovered that happiness doesn't just happen, nor does it have much to do with power, money, or material possessions. "People who control inner experience," he said, "will be able to determine the quality of their lives, which is as close as any of us can come to being happy." In this session, you'll aid participants in exploring biblical truths relating to taking charge of their lives during the second half and discovering the joy that such actions can bring.

Halftime is a time to begin living life out of our core being—out of our internal standards such as character, values, beliefs, and mission—rather than by our work, possessions, accomplishments, and children. Participants will learn key principles and biblical truths that will help them regain control of their destiny.

Participants will be reminded that continuing to learn and grow is more than just a key ingredient of their halftime process. The process of learning and growing should remain a crucial part of their second half. They will have the opportunity to see how a tool Bob Buford used, the Sigmoid Curve, can help them to implement a pattern of learning and growth that will sustain them through life.

Finally, participants will be challenged to keep pursuing what they are passionate about, to tap into their gifts, and to strive to discover their God-given calling so that the rest of their years—the great adventure of the second half—will be the best of their years.

Key Points of This Session

1. Jesus said, "It is more blessed to give than to receive" (Acts 20:35). When we have a dynamic, personal relationship with God through Jesus Christ, we can use our God-given gifts to serve other people, and we'll receive blessedness in return. Nothing we can do is more exciting or significant than partnering with God in a spirit of trust and obedience and using the gifts he has given us to do what he has called us to do on behalf of other people.

2. Halftime is the time to begin living life out of our core being—out of our internal standards such as character, values, beliefs, and mission—rather than by our work, possessions, accomplishments, and children. We can apply proven principles and biblical truths in order to regain control of our lives and experience the significance that comes from living out God's calling.

3. Learning and growing are not just key ingredients of the halftime process. They remain crucial parts of life during the second half. Learning and growing are part of what sustains us through life. As we challenge ourselves to keep pursuing what we are passionate about, tap into our gifts, and seek—with God's help—to discover his calling for each of us, the rest of our years will be the best of our years!

Session Outline (54 minutes)

    I. Introduction (5 minutes)
    Welcome
    What's to Come
    Questions to Think About

    II. Video Presentation: "The Best of Your Years" (15 minutes)

    III. Group Discovery (28 minutes)
    Video Highlights (5 minutes)
    Large Group Exploration (10 minutes)
        Pause for Personal Reflection
    Small Group Exploration (8 minutes)
        Pause for Personal Reflection
    Group Discussion (5 minutes)

    IV. Action Points (5 minutes)

    V. Closing Meditation (1 minute)

Materials

You'll need a VCR, television set, and Bible, but no additional materials. Simply view the video segment prior to leading the session so you are familiar with its main points.

Session

5

The Best of Your Years

To wake up every morning and feel as though you're where God wants you to be that day is as much peace as you're going to find this side of eternity.

Doug Mazza

INTRODUCTION

minutes

Welcome

> Call the participants together. Welcome them to *Halftime* session 5, "The Best of Your Years."

What's to Come

During this session, we'll meet more people from various walks of life who, through the process of halftime, have discovered their God-given calling and are making their second half count. They have discovered the joys of a deeper relationship with God through Jesus Christ and are using their gifts to make a difference in their world. They are living lives of significance, lives of blessedness. We'll be challenged to keep seeking to discover what we are passionate about, to learn to use our gifts in new ways, and to make the rest of our years the best of our years!

Questions to Think About

> Have participants open their Participant's Guide to page 104.
>
> As time permits, ask two or more of the following questions and solicit responses from the participants.

Let's begin our final session by considering a few questions.

 1. During the first four sessions, we considered many aspects of half-time and wrestled with various challenges and issues. How has your

---

Session

5

The Best of Your Years

To wake up every morning and feel as though you're where God wants you to be that day is as much peace as you're going to find this side of eternity.
Doug Mazza

— 105 —

---

104   HALFTIME PARTICIPANT'S GUIDE

QUESTIONS TO THINK ABOUT

1. During the first four sessions, we considered many aspects of halftime and wrestled with various challenges and issues. How has your view of the second half of life changed as a result? Must the second half be a period of decline and decay? Why or why not?

2. What happens to a person when he or she is able to make a significant difference in someone's life?

3. What impact would you like to make during your second half? Why do you think you can or cannot make such an impact?

4. In what ways do you think God can use what has happened during the first half of our lives to prepare us for the second?

view of the second half of life changed as a result? Must the second half be a period of decline and decay? Why or why not?

Possible Answers: Most participants will agree that the halftime sessions have influenced their view of the second half, but the ways in which halftime has influenced them may differ. Encourage participants to express and explain their views. The goal of this question is to stimulate reflection on how the halftime process has, and is, affecting them.

 2. What happens to a person when he or she is able to make a significant difference in someone's life?

Possible Answers: Encourage participants to explore the personal impact—on the giver, not the recipient—that making a difference in someone else's life can have. Responses may include feeling happy or satisfied, realizing how rewarding it is to help someone, being surprised that he or she was able to make a difference, being grateful to God for the opportunity to make a difference.

 3. What impact would you like to make during your second half? Why do you think you can or cannot make such an impact?

Possible Answers: Most of us have a deep longing to make a difference, to do more than achieve fleeting success and then die. Encourage participants to express their longings to the group. At the same time, most of us experience doubt about what we can do. Our reasons for doubt include self-doubt, unwillingness to trust God, not wanting to be disappointed if things don't work out, fear of making necessary changes, etc.

 4. In what ways do you think God can use what has happened during the first half of our lives to prepare us for the second?

Possible Answers: God can use our pain to teach us compassion, our challenges to teach us faith, our relationships to teach us humility and self-control. Our wisdom and financial resources can be shared with other people. Whatever knowledge or experience we have gained can also be applied to second-half endeavors.

Let's keep these ideas in mind as we view the video segment. There is space in your Participant's Guide for taking notes.

QUESTIONS TO THINK ABOUT

1. During the first four sessions, we considered many aspects of halftime and wrestled with various challenges and issues. How has your view of the second half of life changed as a result? Must the second half be a period of decline and decay? Why or why not?

2. What happens to a person when he or she is able to make a significant difference in someone's life?

3. What impact would you like to make during your second half? Why do you think you can or cannot make such an impact?

4. In what ways do you think God can use what has happened during the first half of our lives to prepare us for the second?

PLANNING NOTES

VIDEO PRESENTATION: "The Best of Your Years"

15
minutes

Leader's Video Observations
The pursuit of blessedness

Relinquishing control

Discovering our passion—and going for it!

Making a significant difference

SESSION FIVE: The Best of Your Years 105

VIDEO NOTES

The pursuit of blessedness

Relinquishing control

Discovering our passion—and going for it!

Making a significant difference

PLANNING NOTES

GROUP DISCOVERY

28 minutes

> If your group has seven or more members, use the **Video Highlights** (5 minutes) with the entire group, then complete the **Large Group Exploration** (10 minutes), then break into small groups of three to five people for the **Small Group Exploration** (8 minutes). Finally, bring everyone together for the closing **Group Discussion** (5 minutes).
>
> If your group has fewer than seven members, begin with the **Video Highlights** (5 minutes), then complete both the **Large Group Exploration** (10 minutes) and the **Small Group Exploration** (8 minutes) as a group. Wrap up your discovery time with the **Group Discussion** (5 minutes).

Video Highlights (5 minutes)

> As time permits, ask one or more of the following questions that directly relate to the video segment the participants have just seen.

 1. Bob Buford says, "The only way one can get to blessedness, I'm thoroughly persuaded, is to serve one another with the gifts that God has given us to work with." Do you agree or disagree? Why?

   Possible Answers: Responses may vary. Some people may think that blessedness comes from other sources, too. Some people may think they can achieve blessedness by a route other than serving people. Clearly, though, people who give of themselves to other people receive much in return. [Note: This question reminds participants to think about serving others, to consider such service to be one of many second-half options. What's important is to help participants explore their relationship with God and to reaffirm that God has given each of us specific gifts that will aid us in fulfilling his calling for our lives.]

 2. As the chief operating officer of Hyundai, Doug thought he had it made until his third son, Ryan, was born with severe deformities. Through his suffering, Doug reached the point where he prayed, "Lord, what is it that you would have me do next? I know you have prepared me for something more." What stood out to you as Doug shared his spiritual journey?

   Possible Answers: These will vary. One participant may share how Doug's suffering affected him or her. Another may identify with Doug's belief in Jesus without having a personal relationship with him. Yet another may identify with Doug's desire to try to control life circumstances. Clearly Doug finally relinquished control of his life to God and believed that God had much more in store for him than what he'd seen.

106   HALFTIME PARTICIPANT'S GUIDE

VIDEO HIGHLIGHTS

1. Bob Buford says, "The only way one can get to blessedness, I'm thoroughly persuaded, is to serve one another with the gifts that God has given us to work with." Do you agree or disagree? Why?

2. As the chief operating officer of Hyundai, Doug thought he had it made until his third son, Ryan, was born with severe deformities. Through his suffering, Doug reached the point where he prayed, "Lord, what is it that you would have me do next? I know you have prepared me for something more." What stood out to you as Doug shared his spiritual journey?

3. Why is it important for each of us, like Doug, to step out in faith to find the calling God has for us?

PLANNING NOTES

3. Why is it important for each of us, like Doug, to step out in faith to find the calling God has for us?

Possible Answers: We have to be willing to trust God enough to embark on the great adventure of the second half. We have to relinquish control to God in order to grow into significance. We have to be focused on God and his purpose for us in order to move from externally motivated success to internally motivated significance. The status quo, although easy to maintain, doesn't allow us to reach the potential God has for us.

 4. What attitudes do you see demonstrated in the people interviewed for this video? How successful have they been in encouraging you to find out what you're passionate about and to go for it?

Possible Answers: Responses will vary, but it is clear that life is too short to waste on things that don't matter to us. When we feel passionate about something, we are more motivated and hopeful, energized to take action. So many people coast through their second halves and miss their God-given callings. They remain unfulfilled and long for significance. In contrast, living a life of significance offers excitement and vitality.

Large Group Exploration (10 minutes)

Investing in People

God has given each of us some time, talent, and treasure to invest in fulfilling his two great commandments: "Love the Lord your God with all your heart and with all your soul and with all your mind.... Love your neighbor as yourself" (Matthew 22:37, 39). So as we each begin to chart a new course in life, we may want to think about partnering with God and investing our gifts in service to other people. There is nothing more rewarding than dedicating what we like to do and are good at doing in service to God and people.

 1. More than two thousand years ago, Jesus demonstrated what it means to love people. He taught and ministered to crowds of people under the hot sun and experienced hunger and thirst. He lived in their world and walked their narrow streets. He gave himself—his time, resources, wisdom, knowledge, power, and ultimately his life—for the benefit of other people, even those who hated him. And no one in the history of the world has done anything as significant as he did (and is still doing!).

Let's look up the following verses and see what they reveal about Jesus' love for people and what it means for us to love the people around us—at home, at work, in our communities.

VIDEO HIGHLIGHTS

1. Bob Buford says, "The only way one can get to blessedness, I'm thoroughly persuaded, is to serve one another with the gifts that God has given us to work with." Do you agree or disagree? Why?

2. As the chief operating officer of Hyundai, Doug thought he had it made until his third son, Ryan, was born with severe deformities. Through his suffering, Doug reached the point where he prayed, "Lord, what is it that you would have me do next? I know you have prepared me for something more." What stood out to you as Doug shared his spiritual journey?

3. Why is it important for each of us, like Doug, to step out in faith to find the calling God has for us?

PLANNING NOTES

4. What attitudes do you see demonstrated in the people interviewed for this video? How successful have they been in encouraging you to find out what you're passionate about and to go for it?

LARGE GROUP EXPLORATION

Investing in People

God has given each of us some time, talent, and treasure to invest in fulfilling his two great commandments: "Love the Lord your God with all your heart and with all your soul and with all your mind.... Love your neighbor as yourself" (Matthew 22:37, 39). So as we each begin to chart a new course in life, we may want to think about partnering with God and investing our gifts in service to other people. There is nothing more rewarding than dedicating what we like to do and are good at doing in service to God and people.

1. More than two thousand years ago, Jesus demonstrated what it means to love people. He taught and ministered to crowds of people under the hot sun and experienced hunger and thirst. He lived in their world and walked their narrow streets. He gave himself—his time, resources, wisdom, knowledge, power, and ultimately his life—for the benefit of other people, even those who hated him. And no one in the history of the world has done anything as significant as he did (and is still doing!).

   Let's look up the following verses and see what they reveal about Jesus' love for people and what it means for us to love the people around us—at home, at work, in our communities.

Scripture	How Jesus Loved People in His World	How We Might Love People in Our World
Matthew 8:1–3	*Jesus was already involved with a crowd of people, but he stopped to touch and heal a leper. This showed his great compassion, since lepers were the social outcasts of that time.*	*How deep is our compassion? Will we reach out to the outcasts of our world—the homeless, the sick, the mentally ill, the physically deformed, the addicted—with God's love?*
Matthew 20:29–34	*Jesus stopped what he was doing, went against the cry of the crowd, and did what he was called to do. He listened to the needs of two men whom society wanted to silence, and he healed them.*	*Ministering to people is not always convenient, easy, or respected. Society wants to silence the needy cries of some of its members. When we are busy and pressured, will we slow down enough to listen to and care for the needs of people?*
Luke 5:27–32	*Jesus asked Levi, a tax collector who was hated by the general population and despised by the religious elite, to be his disciple. When the religious leaders complained about his association with sinners, Jesus responded by restating his conviction to meet the needs of hurting and spiritually needy people.*	*We, too, need to stand up for our convictions and not view ourselves as being better than other people. Reaching hurting and spiritually needy people will at times require that we reach beyond our normal associations with people.*
John 8:1–11	*When religious leaders made a public show of an adulterous woman, Jesus was not distracted; he remained focused on the truth and his mission. When the hubbub died down, he looked beyond the outside of the woman and, instead of offering judgment, he touched her heart.*	*It's easy to focus on the externals and to overlook the deep spiritual needs of a person's heart. Yet we love best when we look beyond the outside behavior and appearances and, instead of condemning, steer people toward new life in relationship with God through Jesus Christ.*
John 11:1–6, 17, 32–44	*Jesus closely identified with the pain of other people and often alleviated it through caring words and actions. In this case, he raised Lazarus from the dead not only to alleviate Martha and Mary's pain but also to bring glory to God.*	*It's not easy to carry other people's pain and to stand with them during their suffering, but that is one way we love them. Bringing encouragement and comfort to those who suffer is one way we bring glory to God.*

Scripture	How Jesus Loved People in His World	How We Might Love People in Our World
Matthew 8:1–3		
Matthew 20:29–34		
Luke 5:27–32		
John 8:1–11		
John 11:1–6, 17, 32–44		

2. Let's list some practical ways in which we can use who we are and our resources to demonstrate God's love to other people.

PLANNING NOTES

2. Let's list some practical ways in which we can use who we are and our resources to demonstrate God's love to other people.

Possible Answers: These will vary. The intent here is to encourage participants to see the wide range of opportunities that might fit their gifts and what they are passionate about. These can be anything from holding AIDS and cocaine babies in an intensive care nursery to repairing a single mother's home to starting a job-training ministry for homeless men to helping churchgoers discover and use their spiritual gifts to coaching an inner-city Little League team. The list is endless. Discover what your participants envision.

HALFTIME PERSPECTIVE

Altruistic Egoism

In *Halftime,* Bob Buford mentioned that Hans Selye coined a phrase that sounds contradictory: *altruistic egoism.* It means that helping other people helps you. This truth is nothing new. Long ago, Jesus taught that giving of one's self to other people is actually a form of receiving (Acts 20:35).

Selye noted that people who earn their neighbors' goodwill are dramatically better off psychologically and physically than those who are looked upon as selfish and greedy. He also wrote that the best way to earn the goodwill of your neighbor is to ask either explicitly or implicitly, "What can I do to be useful to you?" And then, if possible, do it.

Pause for Personal Reflection

Now it's time to pause to consider how God may want us to use our gifts and what we are passionate about in loving service to other people.

- If God audibly spoke to me about my mission in life related to people, what would he say? Why?
- Jesus spent the last three years of his life in public ministry, reaching out to people with God's love. In what ways has the first half of my life prepared me, given my options and uniqueness, knowledge and experience, to reach out to other people?
- In what ways might I be able to use what I've been given to serve other people?
- I typically respond to needy, hurting people by _____ _____.
- What does this tell me about my role in serving other people?
- To which people, or group of people, may God be calling me to love and serve in a special way?

Let participants know when there is one minute remaining.

Panel 1 (page 109)

Scripture	How Jesus Loved People in His World	How We Might Love People in Our World
Matthew 8:1–3		
Matthew 20:29–34		
Luke 5:27–32		
John 8:1–11		
John 11:1–6, 17, 32–44		

2. Let's list some practical ways in which we can use who we are and our resources to demonstrate God's love to other people.

Panel 2 (page 110)

HALFTIME PERSPECTIVE

Altruistic Egoism
In *Halftime*, Bob Buford mentioned that Hans Selye coined a phrase that sounds contradictory: *altruistic egoism*. It means that helping other people helps you. This truth is nothing new. Long ago, Jesus taught that giving of one's self to other people is actually a form of receiving (Acts 20:35).

Selye noted that people who earn their neighbors' goodwill are dramatically better off psychologically and physically than those who are looked upon as selfish and greedy. He also wrote that the best way to earn the goodwill of your neighbor is to ask either explicitly or implicitly, "What can I do to be useful to you?" And then, if possible, do it.

Pause for Personal Reflection
Now it's time to pause to consider how God may want us to use our gifts and what we are passionate about in loving service to other people.

If God audibly spoke to me about my mission in life related to people, what would he say? Why?

Panel 3 (page 111)

Jesus spent the last three years of his life in public ministry, reaching out to people with God's love. In what ways has the first half of my life prepared me, given my options and uniqueness, knowledge and experience, to reach out to other people?

In what ways might I be able to use what I've been given to serve other people?

I typically respond to needy, hurting people by _____ _____.

What does this tell me about my role in serving other people?

Panel 4 (page 112)

To which people, or group of people, may God be calling me to love and serve in a special way?

HALFTIME CLIP

This is the true joy in life—the being used for a purpose recognized by yourself as a mighty one, the being a force of nature instead of a feverish, selfish little clod of ailments and grievances, complaining that the world will not devote itself to making you happy. I am of the opinion that my life belongs to the whole community and as long as I live, it is my privilege to do for it whatever I can. I want to be thoroughly used up when I die, for the harder I work, the more I live.
—GEORGE BERNARD SHAW

> *This is the true joy in life—the being used for a purpose recognized by yourself as a mighty one, the being a force of nature instead of a feverish, selfish little clod of ailments and grievances, complaining that the world will not devote itself to making you happy. I am of the opinion that my life belongs to the whole community and as long as I live, it is my privilege to do for it whatever I can. I want to be thoroughly used up when I die, for the harder I work, the more I live.*
> **—GEORGE BERNARD SHAW**

Small Group Exploration (8 minutes)

Living by Our Inner Compass

Bob Buford has observed that "the halftime process of reevaluation is about identifying yourselves by internal standards—your character, your values, your beliefs, your contributions, your mission—rather than by your work, your possessions, your busyness, your children." An internal approach is purpose driven, not driven by external circumstances. This observation echoes the words of Moses in Deuteronomy 30:20. He implored the Israelites to identify themselves by an internal standard, to "love the LORD your God, listen to his voice, and hold fast to him. For the LORD is your life."

A similar sentiment was expressed by Mihaly Csikszentmihalyi, a psychologist who spent twenty-five years trying to figure out what makes people happy. He discovered that happiness doesn't just happen, nor does it have much to do with power, money, or material possessions. "People who control inner experience," he observed, "will be able to determine the quality of their lives, which is as close as any of us can come to being happy."

Since significance and quality of life are such important ingredients in making our second-half years the best of our years, let's consider some biblical passages that call us to exercise discipline over our inner selves and live according to internal standards.

 1. What do the following verses reveal about how we each set our inner compass, how we determine the inner standards that, with God's help, will lead toward a more fulfilled, significant life?

   a. Matthew 6:24–25, 31–34

   Possible Answers: We can't have a split loyalty—we can have only one thing in the box! We can't have a divided heart and mind. We have to choose our inner compass setting. If we choose God, then we aren't to

To which people, or group of people, may God be calling me to love and serve in a special way?

HALFTIME CLIP

This is the true joy in life—the being used for a purpose recognized by yourself as a mighty one, the being a force of nature instead of a feverish, selfish little clod of ailments and grievances, complaining that the world will not devote itself to making you happy. I am of the opinion that my life belongs to the whole community and as long as I live, it is my privilege to do for it whatever I can. I want to be thoroughly used up when I die, for the harder I work, the more I live.
—GEORGE BERNARD SHAW

SESSION FIVE: The Best of Your Years   **115**

SMALL GROUP EXPLORATION

Living by Our Inner Compass

Bob Buford has observed that "the halftime process of reevaluation is about identifying yourselves by internal standards—your character, your values, your beliefs, your contributions, your mission—rather than by your work, your possessions, your busyness, your children." An internal approach is purpose driven, not driven by external circumstances. This observation echoes the words of Moses in Deuteronomy 30:20. He implored the Israelites to identify themselves by an internal standard, to "love the LORD your God, listen to his voice, and hold fast to him. For the LORD is your life."

A similar sentiment was expressed by Mihaly Csikszentmihalyi, a psychologist who spent twenty-five years trying to figure out what makes people happy. He discovered that happiness doesn't just happen, nor does it have much to do with power, money, or material possessions. "People who control inner experience," he observed, "will be able to determine the quality of their lives, which is as close as any of us can come to being happy."

Since significance and quality of life are such important ingredients in making our second-half years the best of our years, let's consider some biblical passages that call us to exercise discipline over our inner selves and live according to internal standards.

1. What do the following verses reveal about how we each set our inner compass, how we determine the inner standards that, with God's help, will lead toward a more fulfilled, significant life?

   a. Matthew 6:24–25, 31–34

PLANNING NOTES

_____

_____

_____

_____

_____

_____

_____

_____

_____

_____

_____

_____

_____

_____

_____

_____

_____

_____

_____

_____

_____

_____

_____

_____

_____

_____

_____

_____

_____

_____

_____

_____

worry and chase after things, such as what we will eat, drink, or wear. Nor are we to love money. Instead, we are to set our compass on pursuing God's kingdom, and he will take care of the rest.

b. Romans 8:5–8

Possible Answers: We can choose where to focus our minds. We can choose to set our minds on external, sinful desires or on that which the Holy Spirit desires. If our intent is to please God, we must set our minds on the desires of the Holy Spirit within us.

 2. It takes discipline to exercise control and live according to our inner compass. Read the instructions given in the following Scripture passages. Note what is said regarding our ability to exercise control over our lives.

a. 1 Timothy 6:12; 2 Timothy 2:1, 3–5

Possible Answers: Paul instructed Timothy to "fight the good fight of the faith." One can't fight a good fight without focus, training, and discipline. Paul then urged Timothy to be strong, to endure hardship and be focused on his area of responsibility like a soldier, and to compete with the discipline of an athlete. These are images of a brawny, manly individual who is pursuing specific goals with single-minded purpose.

b. 1 Corinthians 9:24–27

Possible Answers: The image Paul portrayed is that of a runner whose mind is focused on the goal of winning the race. This person is purposeful rather than aimless and trains to win. Everything other than the runner's goal is put aside.

c. Hebrews 12:1

Possible Answers: Readers are encouraged to eliminate everything external that keeps them from focusing on the goal before them, from running the race God has marked out for them.

d. 1 Peter 1:13–15

Possible Answer: Peter urged his readers to prepare their minds for action, to be self-controlled, to focus their hope fully on Christ, and to be holy in everything. A person who does this will certainly be purpose driven.

b. Romans 8:5–8

2. It takes discipline to exercise control and live according to our inner compass. Read the instructions given in the following Scripture passages. Note what is said regarding our ability to exercise control over our lives.

a. 1 Timothy 6:12; 2 Timothy 2:1, 3–5

b. 1 Corinthians 9:24–27

c. Hebrews 12:1

d. 1 Peter 1:13–15

PLANNING NOTES

3. In light of the passages we've read above, let's talk for a minute about the importance of living by our inner compass and how we go about controlling our inner experiences. What impact do you think living this way will have on our second half? On living a significant life?

Possible Answers: Encourage participants to realize that self-control and a committed focus on what God has called us to do—a focus unaffected by external circumstances—are important elements of the Christian life. Encourage them to express their views and hopes for what living by their internal standards will mean in their lives.

Pause for Personal Reflection

Now it's time to pause to think quietly about our lives and consider how we each set our inner compass.

Lloyd Reeb said, "My real significance at the end of the day is not so much about my effectiveness as it is about my willingness to follow and partner with God where he has called me."

- Is this statement motivated by internal or external standards?
- How would I describe the source of my significance? Is my significance internally or externally motivated?
- On a scale of one to ten, how would I rate my control of my inner experience? What changes do I need to make to better focus my inner compass on things that reflect my true self, the self God created me to be?
- As I look at my daily schedule, is there room in my life for anything else? If not, what do I need to eliminate so that I can carve out more time for things that better represent my core being?

> **Let participants know when there is one minute remaining.**

HALFTIME CLIP

Having a fruitful second half is more than just slowing down or being able to control your date book. It has to do with a mind-set, an inner compass, that is fixed on those things that define the true self.

—BOB BUFORD

3. In light of the passages we've read above, let's talk for a minute about the importance of living by our inner compass and how we go about controlling our inner experiences. What impact do you think living this way will have on our second half? On living a significant life?

Pause for Personal Reflection

Now it's time to pause to think quietly about our lives and consider how we each set our inner compass.

Lloyd Reeb said, "My real significance at the end of the day is not so much about my effectiveness as it is about my willingness to follow and partner with God where he has called me."

Is this statement motivated by internal or external standards?

How would I describe the source of my significance? Is my significance internally or externally motivated?

On a scale of one to ten, how would I rate my control of my inner experience? What changes do I need to make to better focus my inner compass on things that reflect my true self, the self God created me to be?

As I look at my daily schedule, is there room in my life for anything else? If not, what do I need to eliminate so that I can carve out more time for things that better represent my core being?

HALFTIME CLIP

Having a fruitful second half is more than just slowing down or being able to control your date book. It has to do with a mind-set, an inner compass, that is fixed on those things that define the true self.

—BOB BUFORD

PLANNING NOTES

Ten Principles for Regaining Control of Your Life

As Bob Buford pointed out in his book *Halftime,* it's one thing to talk about regaining personal control, yet quite another to really do it. Old habits, even tempered with a brand-new outlook on life, die hard. The following list summarizes how Buford regained control over his destiny. Perhaps some of these principles will apply to you.

1. *Delegate—at work, play, and home.* You cannot do everything and shouldn't try. This is especially important if you keep your present job but do it at half speed so you can express yourself in other ways. Work smarter, not harder.

2. *Do what you do best; drop the rest.* Go with your strengths.

3. *Know when to say no.* The more successful you are, the more you'll be asked to help other people. Don't get talked into doing something you don't want to do or don't have time to do. Pursue your mission, not someone else's.

4. *Set limits.* Cut back on your appointments, your work time, your business trips. Reallocate time to your life mission.

5. *Protect your personal time by putting it on your calendar.* Start your day slowly. It's much easier to maintain control over your life if you have a regular quiet time. A quiet time is more than Bible reading and prayer. Allow time for absolute silence, for deliberately looking at your life to see if it's in balance.

6. *Work with people you like.* As much as possible, work with people who add energy to life, not those who take energy away.

7. *Set timetables.* Your life mission is important, deserving of your attention and care. Second-half dreams that are not put on a timetable quickly become unfulfilled wishes.

8. *Downsize.* To what extent are your time and energy being drained by owning a boat, a cottage, a third car, or a country club membership? None of these things are bad in and of themselves, but if these things stand between you and regaining control of your life, get rid of them.

9. *Play more often.* Play ought to be a big second-half activity, not so much in terms of time spent, but in importance. Play will remind you who's in charge.

10. *Take the phone off the hook.* Learn how to hide gracefully. Unless you're a brain surgeon on twenty-four-hour call, it's not necessary to let people know where you are all the time. Answering machines and voice mail allow us to control who we talk with—and when.

HALFTIME TIP

Ten Principles for Regaining Control of Your Life

As Bob Buford pointed out in his book *Halftime,* it's one thing to talk about regaining personal control, yet quite another to really do it. Old habits, even tempered with a brand-new outlook on life, die hard. The following list summarizes how Buford regained control over his destiny. Perhaps some of these principles will apply to you.

1. *Delegate—at work, play, and home.* You cannot do everything and shouldn't try. This is especially important if you keep your present job but do it at half speed so you can express yourself in other ways. Work smarter, not harder.

2. *Do what you do best; drop the rest.* Go with your strengths.

3. *Know when to say no.* The more successful you are, the more you'll be asked to help other people. Don't get talked into doing something you don't want to do or don't have time to do. Pursue your mission, not someone else's.

4. *Set limits.* Cut back on your appointments, your work time, your business trips. Reallocate time to your life mission.

5. *Protect your personal time by putting it on your calendar.* Start your day slowly. It's much easier to maintain control over your life if you have a regular quiet time. A quiet time is more than Bible reading and prayer. Allow time for absolute silence, for deliberately looking at your life to see if it's in balance.

6. *Work with people you like.* As much as possible, work with people who add energy to life, not those who take energy away.

7. *Set timetables.* Your life mission is important, deserving of your attention and care. Second-half dreams that are not put on a timetable quickly become unfulfilled wishes.

Continued on next page...

8. *Downsize.* To what extent are your time and energy being drained by owning a boat, a cottage, a third car, or a country club membership? None of these things are bad in and of themselves, but if these things stand between you and regaining control of your life, get rid of them.

9. *Play more often.* Play ought to be a big second-half activity, not so much in terms of time spent, but in importance. Play will remind you who's in charge.

10. *Take the phone off the hook.* Learn how to hide gracefully. Unless you're a brain surgeon on twenty-four-hour call, it's not necessary to let people know where you are all the time. Answering machines and voice mail allow us to control who we talk with—and when.

HALFTIME PERSPECTIVE

Three Truths to Remember

1. *What we become during the second half has already been invested during the first half.* We don't have to worry about trying to recreate ourselves. We can examine where we've been and would like to go, and build on our experiences, talents, and knowledge in pursuing our God-given calling.

2. *We don't need to chase things outside of ourselves for fulfillment.* Many people have pursued power, money, possessions, status, and the like, believing that these things would lead to significance. But what's really important is knowing God through a personal relationship with Jesus Christ, discovering the calling God has for each of us, and receiving the blessedness that comes from serving other people.

3. *God doesn't waste what he has created.* God created each of us just the way we are! He desires that we serve him by being who we are and using what he has given us to work with. Not only that, he offers us his love, wisdom, guidance, and strength—all the ingredients we need for a significant second half.

PLANNING NOTES

Three Truths to Remember

1. *What we become during the second half has already been invested during the first half.* We don't have to worry about trying to recreate ourselves. We can examine where we've been and would like to go, and build on our experiences, talents, and knowledge in pursuing our God-given calling.

2. *We don't need to chase things outside of ourselves for fulfillment.* Many people have pursued power, money, possessions, status, and the like, believing that these things would lead to significance. But what's really important is knowing God through a personal relationship with Jesus Christ, discovering the calling God has for each of us, and receiving the blessedness that comes from serving other people.

3. *God doesn't waste what he has created.* God created each of us just the way we are! He desires that we serve him by being who we are and using what he has given us to work with. Not only that, he offers us his love, wisdom, guidance, and strength—all the ingredients we need for a significant second half.

Group Discussion (5 minutes)

Now it's time to wrap up our discovery time. As we complete this series today, let's talk about how we can play the second half of our lives for all we're worth.

> Give participants a moment to transition from their thoughtfulness and begin sharing their observations with the entire group. Use the following questions as discussion starters.

 1. In what ways has your view of yourself and your role in the second half of your life changed since we began this study?

I like to think of halftime as an opportunity, sort of a renaissance. Listen, learn, and do it! The worst you could do is to have to try again.
—RENA PEDERSON

8. *Downsize.* To what extent are your time and energy being drained by owning a boat, a cottage, a third car, or a country club membership? None of these things are bad in and of themselves, but if these things stand between you and regaining control of your life, get rid of them.

9. *Play more often.* Play ought to be a big second-half activity, not so much in terms of time spent, but in importance. Play will remind you who's in charge.

10. *Take the phone off the hook.* Learn how to hide gracefully. Unless you're a brain surgeon on twenty-four-hour call, it's not necessary to let people know where you are all the time. Answering machines and voice mail allow us to control who we talk with—and when.

HALFTIME PERSPECTIVE

Three Truths to Remember

1. *What we become during the second half has already been invested during the first half.* We don't have to worry about trying to recreate ourselves. We can examine where we've been and would like to go, and build on our experiences, talents, and knowledge in pursuing our God-given calling.

2. *We don't need to chase things outside of ourselves for fulfillment.* Many people have pursued power, money, possessions, status, and the like, believing that these things would lead to significance. But what's really important is knowing God through a personal relationship with Jesus Christ, discovering the calling God has for each of us, and receiving the blessedness that comes from serving other people.

3. *God doesn't waste what he has created.* God created each of us just the way we are! He desires that we serve him by being who we are and using what he has given us to work with. Not only that, he offers us his love, wisdom, guidance, and strength—all the ingredients we need for a significant second half.

GROUP DISCUSSION

1. In what ways has your view of yourself and your role in the second half of your life changed since we began this study?

HALFTIME CLIP

I like to think of halftime as an opportunity, sort of a renaissance. Listen, learn, and do it! The worst you could do is to have to try again.
—RENA PEDERSON

2. We've learned a lot about ourselves during our times together. Yet what we've learned is just the beginning. Continuing to learn and grow is a crucial part not only of our halftime experience but also of our second half. Learning and growing are key ingredients in making the rest of our years the best of our years.

In what ways may we need to learn and grow during our second half? In what ways is the learning process different during our second half than it was during our first half? How do we go about learning during our second half?

PLANNING NOTES

2. We've learned a lot about ourselves during our times together. Yet what we've learned is just the beginning. Continuing to learn and grow is a crucial part not only of our halftime experience but also of our second half. Learning and growing are key ingredients in making the rest of our years the best of our years.

In what ways may we need to learn and grow during our second half? In what ways is the learning process different during our second half than it was during our first half? How do we go about learning during our second half?

 3. Bob Buford used the Sigmoid Curve to illustrate a pattern of learning and growth that will sustain us through life. (See Halftime Perspective: Overlapping Curves of Growth on page 194.) Why is it so important for each of us to assess how we use our time and other resources and to start a new curve before the last one peters out?

HALFTIME CLIP

The mistake most people make when they move into the second half is to rely on good intentions. If, at some point, you become discouraged by lack of progress in your life mission, it is possible that you simply may not have gained the knowledge and information necessary to support your dream. . . . In many ways, everything that you do in the second half is a form of learning. That is because learning is really just adopting an attitude of discovery. Expect to learn from everything you approach and don't get too hung up on trying to formalize your study.

—**BOB BUFORD**

120   HALFTIME PARTICIPANT'S GUIDE

3. Bob Buford used the Sigmoid Curve to illustrate a pattern of learning and growth that will sustain us through life. (See Halftime Perspective: Overlapping Curves of Growth on page 121.) Why is it so important for each of us to assess how we use our time and other resources and to start a new curve before the last one peters out?

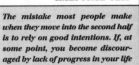

HALFTIME CLIP

The mistake most people make when they move into the second half is to rely on good intentions. If, at some point, you become discouraged by lack of progress in your life mission, it is possible that you simply may not have gained the knowledge and information necessary to support your dream.... In many ways, everything that you do in the second half is a form of learning. That is because learning is really just adopting an attitude of discovery. Expect to learn from everything you approach and don't get too hung up on trying to formalize your study.

—BOB BUFORD

PLANNING NOTES

Overlapping Curves of Growth

Everything, according to Bob Buford, conspires to keep us where we are. That is why so many people remain stuck in the first half or, at best, flounder in a perpetual halftime. Life seems more comfortable in known, familiar territory, even when it bores us to tears and we are fairly certain something better awaits us out there.

How can we overcome this holding pattern? Charles Handy, in his book *The Age of Paradox*, offers a solution: to keep learning and growing into something new. He illustrates this growth pattern in what he has labeled the Sigmoid Curve (see diagram).

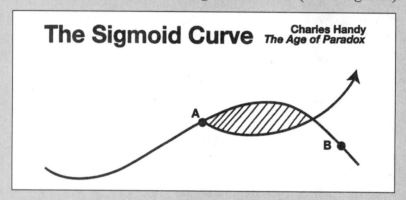

"The secret to constant growth," Handy says, "is to start a new Sigmoid Curve before the first one peters out. The right place to start that second curve is at Point A, where there is the time, as well as the resources and energy, to get the new curve through its initial explorations and flounderings before the first curve begins to dip downward."

The normal pattern for most people, according to Buford, is a single curve that rises as we approach middle age, then sharply drops off toward retirement. A much better approach to life is to have a series of overlapping curves, each one beginning before the previous curve is played out. Buford describes the overlapping curves of his life like this:

The First Curve	The Second Curve
school	apprentice work
apprentice work	doing work
doing work	leading work
leading work	doing ministry
doing ministry	leading ministry
leading ministry	portfolio of ministries

Where are you right now? Are you stuck in one place? Are you just doing time while your first curve drops off? Don't wait to be finished with what you are doing before you start the next curve. You'll always have reasons to stay put. It is faith that calls you to move on.

HALFTIME PERSPECTIVE

Overlapping Curves of Growth

Everything, according to Bob Buford, conspires to keep us where we are. That is why so many people remain stuck in the first half or, at best, flounder in a perpetual halftime. Life seems more comfortable in known, familiar territory, even when it bores us to tears and we are fairly certain something better awaits us out there.

How can we overcome this holding pattern? Charles Handy, in his book *The Age of Paradox*, offers a solution: to keep learning and growing into something new. He illustrates this growth pattern in what he has labeled the Sigmoid Curve (see diagram).

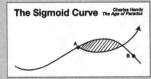

"The secret to constant growth," Handy says, "is to start a new Sigmoid Curve before the first one peters out. The right place to start that second curve is at Point A, where there is the time, as well as the resources and energy, to get the new curve through its initial explorations and flounderings before the first curve begins to dip downward."

The normal pattern for most people, according to Buford, is a single curve that rises as we approach middle age, then sharply drops off toward retirement. A much better approach to life is to have a series of overlapping curves, each one beginning before the previous curve is played out. Buford describes the overlapping curves of his life like this:

The First Curve	The Second Curve
school	apprentice work
apprentice work	doing work
doing work	leading work
leading work	doing ministry
doing ministry	leading ministry
leading ministry	portfolio of ministries

Where are you right now? Are you stuck in one place? Are you just doing time while your first curve drops off? Don't wait to be finished with what you are doing before you start the next curve. You'll always have reasons to stay put. It is faith that calls you to move on.

ACTION POINTS

minutes

The following points are reproduced on page 125 of the Participant's Guide.

As we conclude this series, I'd like to take a moment to summarize the key points we explored today. After I have reviewed these points, I will give you a moment to consider what you will commit to do as a result of what you have discovered during this session.

Read the following points and pause afterward so participants can consider and write out their commitments.

 1. Jesus said, "It is more blessed to give than to receive" (Acts 20:35). When we have a dynamic, personal relationship with God through Jesus Christ, we can use our God-given gifts to serve other people, and we'll receive blessedness in return. Nothing we can do is more exciting or significant than partnering with God in a spirit of trust and obedience and using the gifts he has given us to do what he has called us to do on behalf of other people.

   Carefully think through the people God has brought into your life with whom you have a special desire to share your talents, knowledge, wisdom, etc.

   What practical steps can you begin taking to explore your options for giving of yourself to other people?

 2. Halftime is the time to begin living life out of our core being—out of our internal standards such as character, values, beliefs, and mission—rather than by our work, possessions, accomplishments, and children. We can apply proven principles and biblical truths in order to regain control of our lives and experience the significance that comes from living out God's calling.

   Spend some quiet time during the coming weeks drawing closer to God. Focus on knowing God, discovering who he made you to be, and seeking his will for your life through Bible reading, prayer, and discussions with other Christians.

   Begin writing out the decisions you can make, the steps of faith you can take that will help you take charge of your inner life.

ACTION POINTS

What will you commit to do as a result of what you have discovered during this session?

1. Jesus said, "It is more blessed to give than to receive" (Acts 20:35). When we have a dynamic, personal relationship with God through Jesus Christ, we can use our God-given gifts to serve other people, and we'll receive blessedness in return. Nothing we can do is more exciting or significant than partnering with God in a spirit of trust and obedience and using the gifts he has given us to do what he has called us to do on behalf of other people.

   Carefully think through the people God has brought into your life with whom you have a special desire to share your talents, knowledge, wisdom, etc.

   What practical steps can you begin taking to explore your options for giving of yourself to other people?

2. Halftime is the time to begin living life out of our core being—out of our internal standards such as character, values, beliefs, and mission—rather than by our work, possessions, accomplishments, and children. We can apply proven principles and biblical truths in order to regain control of our lives and experience the significance that comes from living out God's calling.

   Spend some quiet time during the coming weeks drawing closer to God. Focus on knowing God, discovering who he made you to be, and seeking his will for your life through

   Bible reading, prayer, and discussions with other Christians.

   Begin writing out the decisions you can make, the steps of faith you can take that will help you take charge of your inner life.

   If you have not accepted Jesus Christ as your Lord and Savior, talk with a Christian friend or local pastor to learn more about how you can have a personal relationship with God.

3. Learning and growing are not just key ingredients of the halftime process. They remain crucial parts of life during the second half. Learning and growing are part of what sustains us through life. As we challenge ourselves to keep pursuing what we are passionate about, tap into our gifts, and seek—with God's help—to discover his calling for each of us, the rest of our years will be the best of our years!

   Compare your life's curves to a Sigmoid Curve. Are you stuck in the first half? Are you on the verge of a downward slide? Are you on the upward slope of a new curve?

   Identify where you are on your present curve and consider when you need to begin the next curve. Describe what the focus of that learning and growth curve will be.

PLANNING NOTES

If you have not accepted Jesus Christ as your Lord and Savior, talk with a Christian friend or local pastor to learn more about how you can have a personal relationship with God.

 3. Learning and growing are not just key ingredients of the halftime process. They remain crucial parts of life during the second half. Learning and growing are part of what sustains us through life. As we challenge ourselves to keep pursuing what we are passionate about, tap into our gifts, and seek—with God's help—to discover his calling for each of us, the rest of our years will be the best of our years!

Compare your life's curves to a Sigmoid Curve. Are you stuck in the first half? Are you on the verge of a downward slide? Are you on the upward slope of a new curve?

Identify where you are on your present curve and consider when you need to begin the next curve. Describe what the focus of that learning and growth curve will be.

HALFTIME CLIP

Eventually your first half will end. The clock will run out. If it happens unexpectedly—if you do not take responsibility for going into halftime and ordering your life so that your second half is better than the first, you will join the ranks of those who are coasting their way to retirement. . . . But if you take responsibility for the way you play out the rest of the game, you will begin to experience the abundant life that our Lord intended for you.

—BOB BUFORD

CLOSING MEDITATION

minutes

Dear God, how thankful we are for your love and faithfulness to us as we journey into the second half of our lives. We have learned so much during this series, and yet in other ways we have only scratched the surface. Please give us your wisdom and guidance. Just as you have guided other people like us toward significance, guide us so that our second half will be more than just a downward slide toward retirement. We want our second half to count. In Jesus' name we pray, amen.

124   HALFTIME PARTICIPANT'S GUIDE

Bible reading, prayer, and discussions with other Christians.

Begin writing out the decisions you can make, the steps of faith you can take that will help you take charge of your inner life.

If you have not accepted Jesus Christ as your Lord and Savior, talk with a Christian friend or local pastor to learn more about how you can have a personal relationship with God.

3. Learning and growing are not just key ingredients of the halftime process. They remain crucial parts of life during the second half. Learning and growing are part of what sustains us through life. As we challenge ourselves to keep pursuing what we are passionate about, tap into our gifts, and seek—with God's help—to discover his calling for each of us, the rest of our years will be the best of our years!

Compare your life's curves to a Sigmoid Curve. Are you stuck in the first half? Are you on the verge of a downward slide? Are you on the upward slope of a new curve?

Identify where you are on your present curve and consider when you need to begin the next curve. Describe what the focus of that learning and growth curve will be.

SESSION FIVE: The Best of Your Years   **125**

HALFTIME CLIP

Eventually your first half will end. The clock will run out. If it happens unexpectedly—if you do not take responsibility for going into halftime and ordering your life so that your second half is better than the first, you will join the ranks of those who are coasting their way to retirement.... But if you take responsibility for the way you play out the rest of the game, you will begin to experience the abundant life that our Lord intended for you. **—BOB BUFORD**

HALFTIME TIP

Three Principles for Living Out the Best of Your Years
Peter Drucker, noted business writer and consultant, taught Bob Buford three cardinal principles that have helped him keep control over his life:

1. *Build on the islands of health and strength.* You'll build independence rather than dependence.

2. *Work only with those who are receptive to what you are trying to do.* Sure, situations arise in which you can't always do this. But remember, you have only a limited amount of time. Trying to convince people to do what they don't want to do uses four times the energy required to help someone conceive or implement their own ideas.

3. *Work only on things that will make a great deal of difference if you succeed.*

PLANNING NOTES

Three Principles for Living Out the Best of Your Years

Peter Drucker, noted business writer and consultant, taught Bob Buford three cardinal principles that have helped him keep control over his life:

1. *Build on the islands of health and strength.* You'll build independence rather than dependence.

2. *Work only with those who are receptive to what you are trying to do.* Sure, situations arise in which you can't always do this. But remember, you have only a limited amount of time. Trying to convince people to do what they don't want to do uses four times the energy required to help someone conceive or implement their own ideas.

3. *Work only on things that will make a great deal of difference if you succeed.*

A Final Challenge

When I look across the Christian landscape in America, I see a powerful reservoir of energy just waiting to be unleashed. I see enough talent, creativity, compassion, money, and strength to transform our culture.... Yet the church will never have credibility in the community at large without *expressed* individual responsibility. People need to *see* our faith, not merely hear about it.

When our beliefs are personal and privatized, practiced only inside a building once a week, we Christians miss out on that glorious opportunity to be salt and light. Worse, I believe that when faith continues to be directed inward, we become one-dimensional, uninteresting, and wholly self-centered persons.

In the final analysis, you alone must choose how you want to live. You have the freedom to decide whether or not you want the rest of your years to be the *best* of your years. My prayer for you is that you will have the courage to live the dreams God has placed within you.

See you after the game.

—*Bob Buford*

HALFTIME CLIP

Eventually your first half will end. The clock will run out. If it happens unexpectedly—if you do not take responsibility for going into half-time and ordering your life so that your second half is better than the first, you will join the ranks of those who are coasting their way to retirement.... But if you take responsibility for the way you play out the rest of the game, you will begin to experience the abundant life that our Lord intended for you. **—BOB BUFORD**

HALFTIME TIP

Three Principles for Living Out the Best of Your Years
Peter Drucker, noted business writer and consultant, taught Bob Buford three cardinal principles that have helped him keep control over his life:

1. *Build on the islands of health and strength.* You'll build independence rather than dependence.

2. *Work only with those who are receptive to what you are trying to do.* Sure, situations arise in which you can't always do this. But remember, you have only a limited amount of time. Trying to convince people to do what they don't want to do uses four times the energy required to help someone conceive or implement their own ideas.

3. *Work only on things that will make a great deal of difference if you succeed.*

HALFTIME PERSPECTIVE

A Final Challenge
When I look across the Christian landscape in America, I see a powerful reservoir of energy just waiting to be unleashed. I see enough talent, creativity, compassion, money, and strength to transform our culture.... Yet the church will never have credibility in the community at large without *expressed* individual responsibility. People need to *see* our faith, not merely hear about it.

When our beliefs are personal and privatized, practiced only inside a building once a week, we Christians miss out on that glorious opportunity to be salt and light. Worse, I believe that when faith continues to be directed inward, we become one-dimensional, uninteresting, and wholly self-centered persons.

In the final analysis, you alone must choose how you want to live. You have the freedom to decide whether or not you want the rest of your years to be the *best* of your years. My prayer for you is that you will have the courage to live the dreams God has placed within you.

See you after the game.

—Bob Buford

PLANNING NOTES

Video Credits

Written and produced by
John Grooters
Nicole Johnson

Based on the book
Halftime: Changing Your Game Plan from Success to Significance by Bob Buford

Host
Nicole Johnson

Camera and editing
John Grooters

Executive Producer
Mark Hunt

Production Assistants
Mark Klooster
Terry Bowersox
Barb Koorndyk
Linda Bram

The Power of a Moment written and performed by Chris Rice (c) 1998 Clumsy Fly Music. ASCAP. Used by permission.

Seize the Day by Carolyn Arends from the Word Records release I Can Hear You written by Carolyn Arends (c) 1995 Sunday Shoes Music. ASCAP. Benson Music Group, Inc. Nashville, TN. Used by permission.

Please send your comments about this book to us
in care of the address below. Thank you.

ZondervanPublishingHouse
Grand Rapids, Michigan 49530
http://www.zondervan.com